PUBLISHED BY RUSSELL A GRISH

COPYRIGHT MARCH 2013
(Text only)
All rights reserved

PHOTO CREDITS

PHOTOS BY Russell A Grish

GIFTED PHOTOS PGS, 11, 53, 114

GIFTED ART WORK PG. 29 .DARK NATASHA

FILE PHOTOS PGS. 22, 50, 64, 84, 92
(Contributors unknown)

WISE WORDS OF TECUMSEH. www.fistpeople.us

WELCOME

R.A.GRISH

May my journey of purpose be a helpful guide as you navigate the depths of your spirit and wander the Pathways towards your own destination.

WALK IN PEACE

ALONG THE WAY

THE JOURNEY BEGINS 3

THE AWAKENING OF SPIRIT ... 10

THE DARK SIDE 13

THE COMMITMENT 18

CONNECTING 21

THE ROAD GOES ON 91

THE WAY AHEAD 97

THE MEDICINE 28

MY RELATIONS IN NATURE 47

THE EAGLES 63

SPIRITUAL STRENGTHENING 69

THE ROAD CHANGES 82

A JOURNEY OF PURPOSE

THE JOURNEY BEGINS

It's Thanksgiving 1961. I was born the night before. I was the first boy in what was to be a family of four. My mother could not believe that she had a son and asked for her glasses. My father, jubilant, after having three daughters, rushed to the hospital. His face glowed as he held me for the first time.

My mother took me home within the next couple of days. She rode the bus, and on the way she was compelled to stop at her long deceased father's grave. He had died when she was just two, and now she was thirty eight. She held me over his grave and introduced me to him. For many years before in her youth, she would spend afternoons talking, even though she had no memory of him. This was the first stop along the way. I was christened that Christmas Eve.

Growing up with working parents, my first years were spent in the company of old Sicilian women, hair in buns, black dresses and shoes - the smells of traditional cooking, the sounds of their native language. This was my nuna, aunts, their friends and other family members. I could speak and understand their ways before I was able to do so in the language which would be mine.

They would bathe me in the sink, they would feed me cannoli when I cried. It didn't matter what I was crying about - in their loving and caring eyes a cannoli would fix it.

As I grew, I never knew that I was anything other than a chubby Sicilian kid. I didn't see my dad often, or my mother for that matter, being that they were always at work. I was always with these old Sicilian women.

I remember one time, during a severe thunder and lightning storm, my nuna's sister was staying with us. Neither woman spoke English. They both dressed in black, with big shoes and aprons. The aunt wore a black vial, as well, and carried rosary beads. I was upset or crying, and she grabbed me as the thunder and lightning commended. Taking me to a window, she began to pray over me. There were candles lit in the room. From the other room, my nuna yelled out, "He is probably hungry," but to no avail. The aunt insisted that these prayers needed to be said, and said them she did.

On weekends my family would leave the city to go visit with my father's people at Greenwood Lake. His dad and stepmother, brother, sisters and their children would all gather. They would enjoy the weekend's together swimming, boating, playing pool and cards. On one particular weekend, all of the adults were playing cards and drinking. None of the children were allowed to disturb them while they took refuge in my grandfather's man cave. My older cousins and sisters were playing about, me excluded, and I was left un supervised. I was around three years old. Off I wandered to the neighbor's home, who had children also, and a small beach that gave access to the lake.

Almost unnoticed, I walked into the lake. I kept walking until the water was up to about my chest. I couldn't swim at the time and didn't feel like trying to turn around, so I sat down. I could feel myself sitting and not floating on the lake bottom. I felt no fear at all, and actually had a sense of peace and oneness.

I'm not sure if I was breathing but didn't feel out of breath. My eyes were open, and I could see clearly. There was a light all around me. I felt the presence of something there. I felt comfort and can remember smiling as I sat there. I don't know how much time passed, yet I didn't panic.

At some point one of the neighbors children had saw me sitting at the bottom of the lake. He grabbed my head and pulled me up. He told me I could have drowned. I didn't know what that was, so I felt no fear, just peace, protection and at one with the water.

No one paid attention at the man cave when I tried to tell them. It's as if it never happened, but I was there and remember it clearly.

Those weekends went on for some time, and were going on before mine. With the death of my grandfather, it began to change. The last one of those times there that I can remember was also a bit odd. My father had gone to visit his younger sister, who lived just one town over. She had not been feeling well. We, his children, stayed at my grandfather's house. After his visit, he picked us up, and we headed back to the city.

Not far down the road I got a very eerie feeling. I could hear an ambulance coming. We passed the ambulance going in the opposite direction. I stared at it as it went by and continued to do so until it was out of sight. I felt sorrow and sadness and felt the same sadness for my father. I wanted to speak out and tell them, but remained quiet.

When we arrived home, my family received a call informing them that my father's sister, whom he had visited that day, and had appeared to be well, was in the back of that same ambulance. and there she had died.

During the riots of 1967, my family moved from the city just forty miles away. It was Columbus Day.
This new place looked as big as life itself to my young eyes. Rural, safe, no violence just outside the door, no hiding from the windows at night, and the ability to walk to school again without fear. My first order of business in this new land was to get on my bike and explore. I was six at the time

Like usual, off I went on my own to see the sights. I went to the end of the road where a dirt path started and pedaled through the woods. I came to a place where the path grew larger. It was lined with trees that were all bent at the tops forming a tunnel or arch. It was a bit darker in there.

There were streams on both sides of the path, and in my child's mind, seemed to go on forever. Suddenly there was light and the path opened up. My young eyes beheld a large lake. I got off my bike and immediately walked into the water.

This place seemed magical, as did the path that had brought me to it. There were animals and birds, and you could see fish swimming in the shallows.

Large frogs jumped as you would passed by. I stood there, mesmerized, waist deep in the water. In a distance I could see a sailboat. I stared at the boat as it tried to make its voyage, a stare I would learn that I knew from Greenwood Lake. As I stood there, an older kid walked by with a small boat in tow. The boat had the name "skipper" painted on the back. He looked like Ringo Starr. He nodded and said hello as he walked by.

I knew that I should get going home to tell of my adventure. After all nobody knew that I was there. As I headed towards the magical gateway of the path, I felt myself being held back by something, and kept turning to see the sail boat. Finally, when I was about half way home, a fire whistle started to blow. At the time I wasn't sure what that was, but would soon learn.

The very sailboat that I couldn't stop staring at had hit high tension wires strung across the lake with its mast. There were two people in that boat, a father and a son. The son was killed, electrocuted, the father damaged severely.

The kid with the boat, whom I would know for a long time later as "skipper," pulled them from the water, and the fire whistle Was for them.

I would spend a lot of time at this place for many years to follow, connecting to it and to my relations in nature. Going forward I would have other experiences similar to this one involving a swimmer and later a suicide.

In some way reminiscent of the rights of passage, at the age of nine or ten, my father began to instill in me the tools of survival. He would take me along with him, his friends and some relatives, to learn to hunt and fish, to be amongst men, and be able to stand on my own, in his absence,

I was taken out to learn by almost all former soldiers, sailors and marines. At times, I think they forgot that I was a mere child, and they never treated me as one. I spent many days in the woods, at rivers, lakes and on the ocean, and once again found it hard to be near the water without going in and bonding with it.

I went out on hunts and found myself sometimes alone. In those moments I was able to get close to some of the wildlife and always found them or they found me. At times I found myself in large fields of tall grass, forgetting that I had come to hunt. Lying naked in the grass feeling the sun upon me, the breeze around me, smelling the smells of autumn, and feeling as if was a part of it all. This feeling follows me to this very day.

Between the ages of ten and twelve, I got my first gun. A shotgun. Prior to that I hunted with only a knife but did more animal and fish cleaning with it than hunting.

I learned from my father and his brethren there was a code and ethic that needed to be followed, and rules of making a kill.
Looking back, they were good rules and ethics, treating the animals and birds with respect, dignity and allowing them a chance to survive the days hunt.

As I branched out on my own, a pattern was being created. I found all the animals and birds that any hunter would love to. I tried to get them to run or fly, to give them a chance to survive. In most cases they did not. They had no fear and didn't see me as a predator.

Sometimes they would walk right up to me as I held my shotgun in pursuit of them. I would yell to them, "Runaway, I'm here to kill you," yet they would continue to be still, almost as if they were trying to communicate with me.

Going ahead, hunting became a day in the woods for me, to bond with my relations in nature. The shotgun was just a prop to show the public.

I always felt different from others and can never remember ever feeling like a child, more like a seasoned spirit inside a child's life. I always felt protected and never worried that harm would come to me on any level.

I have always felt that I needed to present myself as wise and knowing, even in my earlier years, demonstrating that time and time again.

I always loved women. Girls not so much - women. I never thought about cooties, I thought about women. I smoked, drank and looked at girly books by the age of eight, and hung out with an older crowd before kids my own age.

Guns, tools and barbells were given to me as a child in lieu of toys; this was the way of my father.

At this point, there were many other things and stories to tell, but this is not about a story. I would learn one day that all that happened would become significant to the man I would someday emerge to be. These were the building blocks, the foundation and the tools needed for a long and hard journey that was yet to come.

These were the virtual wires that connected me someday to all things, to every man and woman, to all my relations in nature. These were the beginnings of wisdom and knowledge, life experiences good, bad or otherwise. I learned that all happened for a reason, that there was no coincidence, and that patterns our lives take over the span of time, are in fact, the way it is supposed to be.

We all, as products of creation, have come here with a meaning, a journey and a purpose. Not all will awaken to or recognize that these things are taking place, but it happened for me. These experiences were the introduction to the natural world - the sun, moon, sky, the four elements of creation and my relations in nature. As the journey continued, this was just another stop. Along the way.

THE AWAKENING OF SPIRIT

I always have, since moving from the city, been enchanted by American Indian peoples and their ways, I guess, because of my geographical location, it was the Lenape. The first school field trip I remember was to a local museum. It held a room, dedicated to the ancestors of whose land I dwelt. I couldn't look away when I saw an entire recreated village that had been somewhere close to my home. I felt myself inside that model. A strange familiarity, a sense of belonging, and sadness that I had been there and no longer was. The attraction was overwhelming. My aunt worked at a publishing house and brought me my first book, not knowing of my experience. It was all about American Indians. I loved it, but never truly read it. I looked at the pictures and felt a closeness that I would continue to feel throughout my life. To the present day, I still dwell in Lenapehoking.

The years ahead would be filled with many challenges, so much heartache, sadness and loss of loved ones and personal struggles of trying to fit in and find my place upon this earth and serving my purpose. This purpose was not apparent at the time.

Though things were hard and responsibilities were large to a growing boy and teen, I always prevailed. Again, I never felt that any harm on any level would come to me, and when I stood my ground, I did not stand alone. Many times throughout my teen years and into my early twenties, I found myself in situations that truly could have had tragic outcomes, including death. Each and every time something intervened whether a near overdose, an auto accident or a circumstance or two involving a gun. I never felt danger.

My father had been sick for a very long time. It began with a tractor trailer accident when I was twelve. He was pronounced dead in the ambulance, on the way to the morgue, he began to move - he was alive again! The following years of his life were a struggle to live in the eyes of almost anyone, numerous heart attacks, strokes, loss of limbs, cancer, etc. He died more times than I can count and was brought back each time.

No matter the circumstances of his health, or the de habilitation's that they caused, he would greet each day with a smile and a true appreciation of life, not just his own, but all life. He was the only hero that I ever had.

One time my family received a call from his doctor while he was in the hospital informing us to come see him that very evening. The doctor said that his liver and kidneys were shutting down and he wouldn't be there in the morning. There was no hope. I might have been as young as nineteen or as old as twenty one at the time. I went to be with him immediately. When I arrived he was yellow and weak with a look of "this is it" in his eyes, a look of "my job with you son has not yet been completed, there is much more to learn, I don't want to fail you."

With tears in my eyes, I sat next to him. I prayed like I have never prayed before. I held his hand the entire time. I asked the universe to give him strength and for me to take his sickness. I prayed long and hard, visualizing my energy going into him and his sickness coming to me. 1hiswent on for hours and I was crying the entire time.

My father lived for almost two years after that day. I used this method with him on other occasions, and between his will, my will and the spirits who watched over us both, he survived.
Eventually he fulfilled his journey upon this earth, and was the last of his family to pass. He died a good death with peace and dignity in his home, with the woman he loved by his side.

THE DARK SIDE

Life after the death of my father was a very turbulent time. I felt as if I needed to escape all of the realities that had been my life up to this point. Without going into detail, it was all bad I walked a dark path, the road to hell so to speak. Along the way I met many people who were walking that way as well. For the most part, we were all trying to escape from something. Our time together was meant to be. This was the next stop along the way.

As I tried to navigate my way on this darkened path something inside of me wouldn't allow me to make a full commitment to its less than human mind set. Thoughts of my mother, whom I loved and respected and didn't want to hurt or disappoint and the lessons of my father and the idea that his spirit would be disgusted by his son, whom he would feel he had failed, kept me in check.

little did he know, that most of my young life was spent feeling that I had failed him and that I would never be able to measure up to the kind of man I believed that he was. A real man, content in his skin, tough as nails, a true gentleman, quiet mannered, loved by women and children - kind to our relations in nature, well -received but feared by men, but feared out of respect.

Throughout those years I wound up helping many of those dark dwellers through counseling, rational thought (as rational as one can think under the circumstances) acts of kindness and understanding and generosity to a fault. I learned during this time to walk in two worlds, the light and the dark. This time would also come to serve me on my own spiritual path and my own development in becoming human. Yes kids, we have to develop into human beings!

We are not born that way; we have to walk our paths, learn our lessons and understand the true meaning of what human is. As we get closer, we will evolve and become enlightened. When we are whole, we will ascend. We were created along with all things upon this earth, but yet, we are the most imperfect species of all creation. We lost our way. We lost our connection to the earth and the natural world.

We have severed our personal connection to the Great Spirit, and have left our spiritual beings in the hands of powerful, political, money for redemption organizations who claim that they are the only way to God and peace.

Life on the dark side began to feel as if it were going to go on forever, leaving me feeling hopeless. The only thing that kept me going was, I knew inside that this was all for a reason, that someday it was going to change. Each day and night held a spiritual battle within myself. A love and hate relationship.

I had a plan that began as a young man. This plan included all of the things that one could want in life. A career that paid well, a wife, a home, some kids. However, this was not to be the plan at the time. Perhaps they were only thoughts that might never manifest themselves into reality.

When I stated on an earlier page that it was all bad, it was all bad. Everything that I had attempted to put into motion had failed to take hold, never rooted or flourished. In my soul, I felt all of these things were just not meant to be, that down the road, something was waiting for me that would bring fulfillment, peace and return my self-esteem. There wasn't any direction, none at all, so I sat and waited on a higher call.

Wait is just what I did, turning all that happened on the dark side into a learning experience gathering wisdom and knowledge. Yes there is a lesson to be learned in all behavior, good or bad.

What I found out during this period is that both the good and bad exist in everyone - no one is exempt. The good behavior is obvious to the eye. It has already been established to be what it is. It's easily manufactured and presented for our entertainment.
There is the bad, which also has been determined to be a certain way, and again, is easily identified and not presented but pointed out by the good. What I have come to believe, after walking the journey through the dark as well as the light is, for the most part, being good as we know it, may only exist aesthetically. It's usually those who point out what isn't good who have demons in their heads. Their constant pursuit and desire to be righteous is their own spiritual battle, one they fear can be lost to the dark at any time. The bad do stay bad, but the difference is there are the bad who seem this way because they do not prescribe to the so called norms ,the one size fits all theory of societies that find it okay to kill and destroy, but bad to live in a natural way with true freedom of mind body spirit.

. All things in balance - the light and the dark. The sun and the moon, the sky and the earth. This is the way, the great creators plan. We, as a part of that plan and of creation, need to put ourselves back into balance becoming as one with all things again and to sew ourselves back into the web of life. When man becomes out of balance, the earth follows, and all things upon her as well.

GRANDMOTHER SPIDER

SEWING THE *WEB* OF LIFE

THE COMMITMENT

As all things around me began to come apart (my relationships, my marriage, my sense of who I was and the ugly reality of what I had become) I found myself alone, once again, beaten, and to some extent, tired but ready for the next stop along the way.

Out of sorts and out of options, I took to the road, seeking answers. I separated myself from the influence of the unclean environment that had been created to find myself, somewhere, in America. For the most part, it was a wonderful, soul searching time, revisiting lands that I had traveled to as a young man with my father and mother and meeting more people while traveling solo, no fear, and no issues.

One day, returning from the road, I stopped to say hello to someone I used to know. The visit was cordial and friendly. We caught up on the years since we last spoke, and it was good. I invited her to join me at an upcoming event, and she accepted.

During the affair we laughed, ate and danced. I was invited away from my table to participate in activities that had become the norm to those whom had known me that way. I passed. My company for the evening was on a personal road to recovery, and out of respect, I declined.

We kept company going forward. Occasionally I fell back into the rut of bad behavior, bad at least for me. Still it endured.
Later she would also fall backwards on her journey. I found myself alone again. With nowhere else to go, I went back to the dysfunction of the dark for a bit, but not for long. I needed to understand and accept the circumstances in which this woman found herself. There was something about her, or about me for that matter, which told me that this was the next stop along the way.

I kept close and remained patient, I would tell her that this will soon come to a close. She would look for me, she would need me. After a short time my revelations came to be. I put aside the rest of the things that were occupying my time and went to her side.

My heart and my spirit knew I had to be here where I was. This was the time, and the time was now. This was when all the lessons or (medicine) of the past, would come to flower. The first time we were going to be intimate, she, in a tearing voice, filled with uncertainty and preparation to be humiliated or scoffed and kicked to the curb, told me she was beyond ill in what could possibly be a death sentence. I looked at her and felt all of her emotions touch my heart and my spirit, and I knew that this was the way and my life would become defined by our time together.

My purpose and my place upon the soft and beautiful earth would now become apparent. I answered her, "I will not run away, I don't run away from issues like this. It's not who I am, nor what I do." I embraced her to give her comfort and reassurance. As I looked upon her face I said, "This will be the greatest love that you have ever known."

At that very moment, I made a spiritual commitment with the creator - a commitment to be the man that I was meant to be for my time to shine had arrived.

CONNECTING

Returning to the place where my ancestors once flourished, I felt comfort. I had come here as a child with my father. He told me stories of when he was a boy, how he had been here, and the time he spent with his grandparents. His eyes would grow bright as he spoke of days of grandeur, success and influence.

I also spent time here as a younger man, working and playing, feeling close to the land and the water. The surrounding mountains were prevalent when the sun set and over the water when the sun rose.

This was Lenape land and still recognizable in that way. The grandmothers and grandfather spirits were here living as they once did. Their legends were still told, their names were on surrounding streets, and schools. Having grown up on their land this, too, became another stop along the way.

The town where I grew up had a rich history of Lenape occupation. Lenape villages were abundant as were all things in their time, and traces of their existence scattered the landscape.

Here their presence could be felt. The minds eyes could see why they called this home. The Munsi band, the wolf clan, the people of the rock. I found my place and would tell myself, "I am meant to be here." This place felt like returning home.

Stories have been written about this place. One was about a man named Chincopee and a large bear. The legend says that he returned to the place of his youth long after his people had been driven away from here. He was alone, solo, and would see his life end here where it had begun, dying with the last large bear beside him.

My life as a spiritual man was about to begin. Though the lessons were not close to being over, the application of the knowledge collected (aka the medicine) was to come to be in this place. This was the place of my grandfathers, both by flesh and blood, and by spirit. My commitment was also about to go forward in a strong and rapid way.

My partners' challenges were going to become tougher in those days. The creator and the spirits put me here to help her get through them and to grow on a personal level. The things I had dreamed of when I was a boy, the plan I had made originally for my life would strangely come to be. However, it was not in the aspect of which I thought, nor the fashion, and in a less than conventional manner. None the less, it would happen, and I was ready.

In the short days ahead, my metal would be put to the test. The commitment that I made would prove to be challenging, mostly in the mental realm, yet strengthening my spirituality each day. The ability to share my will and the will which I inherited with others would become apparent as it did so many years ago with my father.

Things began to escalate at a rapid rate concerning the already known condition of my partner. It was obviously taking its toll on her mentally, physically and spiritually. It infected her entire being. She was involved in a couple of support groups to share time and thought with those whom were walking a similar path. She asked me time and again to attend the one for those who are caregiver or family members living with those horrible circumstances.

I agreed eventually and participated with the company of her adult son by her request. The atmosphere there, was alike the atmosphere that had surrounded the other members of her group when I had been in their company previously. The sadness and heavy energy was prevalent and almost overwhelmed me. As I looked into the doors of their spirits (their eyes) and knocked, there seemed to be no one home. There wasn't any shine, no sign of the spiritual life force.

After listening for a while, I was compelled to share my medicine with them and the knowledge and wisdom acquired during my former years. I spoke of the transference of good and clean energy, how not to just accept what is said to be the last word. Through strength of mind and spirit nothing was impossible. Unfortunately it fell upon deaf ears. This was more of a hospice for those who were not going to die. I never returned.

At this point, I sat and spoke to my partner and told her she was not like the others. She had me, and we would overcome any obstacles that would stop her from achieving the life that our creator had wanted her to have.

Sometimes caution is needed when intervening in someone's personal struggle. We don't know why it's happening. It could very well be karmic, meant to be, a lesson that must be learned before evolving to human status. In this particular case, I was guided there for my good and hers. This wasn't going to stop the future medical issues and suffering, but it was going to soften the blow. For she still had much to learn, or to pay for, whether brought on by herself, or by the violations of her forbearers.

I have learned along the way that sometimes an individual or family can carry a spiritual burden with them. An inheritance from their forbearers. Perhaps in the past something took place that violated the laws of the natural world or the laws the creator put forth. This could go on for generations and be passed on like herpes. Like herpes, it may seem to go away for a while and then suddenly makes an encore performance. Sometimes this spiritual matter is passed from spouse to spouse with no blood connection at all. I don't really know why, but I have witnessed it in my own family and the lives of others.

When we put out negative thoughts and energies into the universe by the way we speak and or act towards other human and non-human beings or groups, it can come back to us in ways that we are not able to conceive. Sometimes it can appear as a long running streak of bad luck for a family or group-sickness, heartache, pain and struggle. Perhaps it is an abused person, who continues throughout life attracting abusive people to them and cannot find a way out or eventually finding some type of distorted comfort in that type of circumstance - an addiction, in any shape or form of the word. Circumstances such as poverty and despair, going forward through generations with no hope for change. Poor health, especially when so many from one family unit find themselves affected by the same types of illness, yet medically they aren't genetically inherited. What seems to be an unusual amount of early death, or less than peaceful ways in which one departs this life.

I am not saying by any means that all of these issues are an effect of a spiritual issue, nor that every group of people who suffer these things are a result of that scenario. What I would say however, is that a good percentage of these folks mental or physical issues have roots in this genre.

I found that a self-examination of my life (and asking those of whom I was about to help do the same) was an important part of the healing process. Beginning with recognizing the patterns in their family history and events, the good and bad and the so called coincidental was a good start. Proceeding to recognize the things in their own lives that may have contn1mted to their current state of being, both mentally and physically was the next step, continuing to recall forgotten experiences, encounters, and traumas - personally or witnessed as a child - and perhaps, things on a subconscious level that may have been absorbed by the spirit, to grow and flower later, but unable to identify just who or what had planted the seeds.

Preparing the ground for what was to come I began to make a connection to the land that I was living on. I put new energy into the home of my partner changing and rearranging, cleansing the house of the past and removing the stains on the very fabric of its former existence including memories of what was and instilling the hope of what was to be.

In the beginning I encountered some resistance, but as it flowed and began to take shape, it transformed into a place of peace, healing and sanctuary. It wasn't long before our home would be full. The return of her son and his someday bride, along with other family members and representatives from the animal kingdom. Bringing back the memories and comfort I felt as a boy I was now in my wheel house.

Things were taking hold. The decor began to reflect a tranquil and peaceful environment. We lived together, we laughed together, and we were a tribe. The plans I made for myself as a boy were now rooting and flourishing. None the less there were still many challenges that would present themselves. I grew much stronger, more grounded and connected to my spirit each day. I was becoming the man that I was meant to be, before the light turned into darkness and continued working hard and doing all that was possible to make our home a place for all to be welcome, to come and to find peace and comfort,

My self- prophecy was unfolding before my eyes, and I fought hard to keep the momentum going.

Trying to live life differently and to put out of mind all of the realities that had brought me to this place was the way forward. The animal people came to visit. The earth would respond to the care that I showed for her. People came to celebrate life. We bonded together, and the tribe was large.

Those who gathered were diverse in age and in needs. All, at some time, would leave the village and walk their own journeys, finding their way, purpose, and meeting up with their own challenges. They went forward filled with hope to stay strong and survive.

Needing to continue in the fulfillment of my promise, I felt I had to get right with myself. Many things that began in my youth had not been completed. I began to write, mostly poetry, and paint, sculpt and carve. I kept at it, diligently, as if I were trying to make up for lost time. I turned my energies to music, finding those of like minds that would help bring my words to song. Not much in the sense of finance, or popularity came from these artistic endeavors, but they did bring something that was priceless, something that would last and fuel the future, a real and true sense of accomplishment, both mentally and spiritually.

From this point my journey continued and gathered back things that I lost along the way. I took care of unfinished business, made up for the squandering of talent and ability, and used material items as benchmarks in my pursuit of lost time.

During this time of gathering, the first of many physical ailments, outside of the original, would surface in my partner. Emergency heart surgery was the order of the day. She had been sickly from birth and suffered in the past with heart issues before our time together, but not to this extent. Dealing with the complications of her already well-rooted issues, the operation was a success. She made a full recovery. I stayed by her side during the post-op period and held her hand and prayed for strength for her. "We get to walk together for another day, and it's a good day." In between traumas with my partner, I came upon a friend, who was also having a long and hard journey.

At some point in our relationship, she became ill with a liver disease, and it was one that could prove to be lethal.
There was only one way to treat it. It was as troubling as the disease itself. I stayed informed on her condition, and one day asked her if I could try some things that might help her. She agreed. I used a technique that some native people call "sucking doctor11 which consists of removing poison, real or spiritual by sucking it out of the body orally or through a hollow bone. This was a turning point to the next stop along the way.

THE MEDICINE

I began treating my friend using the sucking medicine. Each time I did I grew sick, not out of commission sick, but sick none the less. I sucked out the spiritual residue near the liver and blew it out into the air. At the time I wasn't aware that there were other procedures and protocol to follow in order to not bring harm to myself. In any case, what doesn't kill you will only make you stronger!

I began to educate myself about pressure points, chakras, and meridians of the body. I knew the spiritual and mental aspects of the human, just not from a traditional sense of learning. I continued to treat her with energy healing techniques, acupressure, massage, native herbs and prayer. This continued for an extended period of time, and I worked with her in a spiritual capacity to help her get back on her path and own personal journey that the Great Spirit had intended for her. There was much to sort out, to accept, to understand and digest, eventually getting past and moving ahead.

The results of our time together proved to be fruitful for her and myself as well. Her affliction was held in check and didn't progress or cause any de habilitation. Her mind, body and spirit became whole and strong and resulted in a centered and grounded person prepared and ready to go ahead to meet the challenges that would arise.

Oh, I didn't mention this, an oversight on my part. I had been told that bears were spotted near my home. I hadn't seen one but knew I must. I prayed to the spirit of the bear to come and visit and share his medicine with me. I waited and waited. One evening I walked outside and sitting there in the place where my future sweat lodge would stand was the bear! I greeted him or her. My heart filled with joy, we looked into each other's eyes as if we were family. When the spirits bring someone to me, it's after an encounter with the bear.

When my friend needed reassurance on her path, the bear sat outside her home. On a hill he watched over her, and on another occasion, sat in her driveway to say hello to her new husband, and let him know that his time to heal had arrived.

My connection to the bear would grow as time passed. They became my medicine, power animal or totem if you will. Prior to this connection with the bear, during the earlier days of my relationship and new home, I noticed one day that three crows sat in a tree outside my kitchen window. I had not mentioned this to my partner. It was always on a Sunday morning that they caught my attention. I asked her if she had noticed this as well. She replied that she did, and always on a Sunday morning. "What do you think they want?" I asked her.

Now that I was aware of them, I noticed them every Sunday morning in the tree outside my kitchen window. They seemed to be very patient. After observing them for some time, I came to the conclusion that they came for a reason and wanted to be noticed and acknowledged and had something to share with me. One morning I decided to acknowledge them out loud and said "Good morning," and waved to them from the window. They in turn, one at a time, moved their heads up and down as if to nod. Then they walked to the end of the branch, again, one at a time, and flew off. This was the beginning of a long time kinship and connection with the crows and their raven cousins.

Sometime earlier a similar experience came with a family of raccoons. I was up long before dawn, readying myself for work and heard something outside my kitchen on our deck. We had a garbage pail out there for some reason, but it usually it was not. I stepped outside and could barely see. I heard something and reached inside to turn on a light. Behold, a raccoon family had come to feast! As surprised as I was, they were also. We looked at each other without any fear and with mutual respect. Some sat on the rail of the deck and one or two were still in the garbage can peeking out.

Eventually they were all out on the rail. We stood there, looking at each other, and then I spoke to them. First I complimented them on their size and appearance, then quietly let them know that this wasn't a good thing, and they were going to wake up everybody in the house. We were no more than a couple of feet from each other, and they looked at me as if they understood every word that I said. The expressions on their faces were like those of children getting caught with their hand in the cookie jar. They departed, quietly and slowly, doing the walk of shame. One would stop and stand up gesturing with his head back towards the feast he had to leave behind, With a smile, and a too cute laugh I said, "No Rocky - sorry, you have had enough." The raccoons never bothered my garbage again. In later years one tried and I caught him before he was able to climb in. He also had that same childlike expression on his face. We spoke and I told him if he would leave the garbage alone I would get him some food. He climbed a tree close by and sat on a low branch waiting for me to return, holding up my end of the deal. My relationship with the raccoons would continue on. I love them.

"If you talk to the animals they will talk to you, and you will know each other. If you don't talk to them you will not know them and what you do not know you will fear." Chief Dan George.

THREE CROWS........THE RACOONS

Connecting with our relations in nature is a key and a vital step to finding oneness with all things as well as ourselves. Nature has so much to teach us and so much to share as well. Again all things in nature have a power, purpose and reason that fit into a perfect plan of balance upon the earth. The plants, trees, animals, birds, rocks, bugs, all that walk, crawl, fly, swim, seen and unseen. Opening your mind and spirit to this concept will bring proof of its existence - visual proof.

All of our relations in nature bring with them a message and a lesson for us. They speak to our spirits, to our thoughts, circumstances and situations. They represent things that may be going on in our lives, our struggles, our quest for understanding and truth. For nature is perfect and cannot be duplicated no matter how intelligent we as a species are. They hold the original knowledge, from the time they could speak as we.

The lessons of survival early man learned from our relations in nature. From hunting, to which things were good to eat, medicine from plants, the weather, community and leadership. Some of the prophets in major religions were surrounded by animals at their inception or used them to carry their message forward. The Catholic Church has a saint dedicated to our relations in nature. God ...The creator...The great spirit or whatever your culture may refer to it as wants it to be this way. In the beginning he put all of these things here first. He seeded the earth with all things that his less than perfect creation would need to survive: food, shelter and clothing from animals; medicinal plants, as well as the edible; and clean clear water. All things in perfect balance, each with its own purpose and reason, even the things that we cannot find reason for or purpose, maybe here to keep us in check, as challengers, or, possibly, just to be a pain in the ass.

For me, the bond has been re-established with all of these things. In my daily prayers they are mentioned - first the Creator, then the four powers of the universe (the four elements of creation) mother earth, all my relations in nature, and finally the ancestor spirits.

The day that the twin towers fell, I was laid off from my job. My partner was in the hospital and had developed some type of virus or infection. I went there to be with her every day, praying for her, and advocating on her behalf while I prayed. After a couple of days in the hospital, being treated for this infection or virus, things continued to decline. The doctors were unable to identify the cause or type of virus. They wanted to equate it to her original condition, but those doctors who had been treating her for that, had never seen this before. She was on so much medication, mostly strong antibiotics. Still no progress was being made. Her condition was worsening, she was completely out of sorts, almost delirious, and wasting away. About five days in, we met with her doctor, and he said that they still couldn't identify what was happening. Many tests had been run yet they were perplexed by the results .they began with flu like symptoms and grew worse as time passed. Spinal taps, x rays, multitudes of blood tests, cultures, and still no results.

With one hand I would sit each day and hold her, and with the other, wipe the tears from my eyes as I watched the horror of what was 9/11unfolding on television, sad and sickened by this event in time. Life would never be the same again, not just for me but for all people. A beginning of the end feeling rang through my mind and spirit.

I stayed by her side each day and into the night. She had a reputation for being a difficult patient. I needed to be there with her to regulate her behavior and speak on her behalf. Six or seven days into her infirment, she lay there, completely out of it, moaning and shaking, repeatedly saying that she was freezing, and yet unresponsive to questions.

In the eyes of those around her, including the staff at the hospital, we were losing her. There didn't appear to be way forward.

The prognosis looked grim. I had seen this scenario in the past, and it was all too familiar. I made a determination that I needed to intervene. I crawled into the bed with her, embraced her, prayed, and shared my energy with her. I lay there for quite some time, never letting my grip on her falter, visualizing her recovery, feeling the warmth of energy engulfing her, and the warmth of love filling her spirit. The shaking stopped. The moaning stopped. She found rest, peace and comfort.

The next day, she began to eat, drink and become more lucid, awakening from a coma, so to speak. No memory of all the days that had passed. The suffering ceased.

On the second day, her vital signs were stabilized, appetite somewhat normal, discomfort gone. The doctors came in and said that they weren't sure what had happened, or even what this all was or what may have caused it. She was going to be released from the hospital and their care within a day or so.

To this very day, no one knows what had happened and why it turned itself around -- no one but me.

With the road to another recovery behind us, we set forth. Going forward there would be many more episodes of sickness and recovery that would baffle the physicians of whose care she was in.

One of the many stories that I would like to share came a couple of years later. Mind you, the ball began rolling at the inception of this relationship when the announcement of her current health status was revealed. The damage that had been done prior to our union had already taken its toll on her mentally, physically and spiritually. From the time of her birth, she had heart problems that would stay with her throughout her life.
Dysfunctional behavior and its effects would also weigh upon her being later down the road. The revelations that surfaced, dealing with abuse mentally, physically and sexually would, forever, leave deep scars on her spirit and continually come back to haunt her throughout her life. This time she was at her work, feeling very ill and experiencing sharp pains near her abdomen. With not a thought in her head to bring herself to the hospital or, for that matter, ask a co-worker or call an ambulance, she drove herself to the home of my mother who lived nearby. She was in excruciating pain. I got a call from my family that she was there and what the circumstances were. I asked them to take her to the hospital, but she refused to go. She got on the phone and told me to come to my mother's house. I, again, told her to go to the hospital, and again, she refused. My mother lived about twenty

minutes away, and it felt as if it took only ten to get there. When I arrived, she was on the couch holding her stomach, crying and in pain. "Let's go," I said, "time for the hospital," and in her childlike manner she cried harder and refused. I had her kneel on the couch. I began using my hands to put energy into the afflicted area, moving them back and forth and in a circular motion, all the time concentrating on the area. "I think it's your appendix," I told her. "You need to go to the hospital." Again, she refused. I continued to work on her, and the pain began to subside. I made her eat and drink to induce vomiting, and vomit she did, but it wasn't right. It looked wrong. After some time had passed, she seemed to gain her composure. We headed for home.

The rest of the evening she spent sleeping, eating very little, drinking a bit. Again, I suggested she go to the hospital, but she still refused. We came to a compromise - if she wasn't feeling better by morning, she would go to the hospital.

The morning came. Upon her awakening, I asked if she felt any better. She stated, "Somewhat, but still not well this time, no more negotiations, and off we went. After being admitted, tests done and all of the usual, the doctors came to the conclusion that her appendix needed to be removed. It was an emergency surgery done at night. Upon completion, the surgeon came out to speak with us. He said that all went well, but what was unusual to him, however, was something he had never seen before- her appendix had perforated. Some of the poison was able to get into her body, yet, somehow, had turned and managed to seal itself off by lying against an intestine. This stopped the leak and saved her from toxicity. Due to length of time she refused to go to the hospital, it saved her life as well. "Hmmm," he muttered as he departed.

Many instances like this one would happen in the coming years, not only with my partner, but again, within my own family.

Case in point: I have three sisters. We all grew up in the same household with the same parents. Though I am sure they had things of a spiritual nature happen to them, I'm not quite sure that they even thought to connect the dots, so to speak, or to make an assessment of what was happening to and around them, if there was a reason why things were taking place. Each of them suffered in their personal lives, whether it be a matter of health, loss of spouse, finances, or issues with their children. They witnessed many of the same events that had taken place in our home regarding my father's health and were visited by spirits in dreams or in person. Some felt as if they were being tormented inside by something they couldn't acknowledge.

We were well aware of our family's history, of early death, the whole riches to rags thing, of struggle. Yet, as the years progressed, they also fell into the circle of our forbearers' plight.

My father's mom died at the age of forty three. She had been divorced from my grandfather at the time. His mother died even younger. He was estranged from his father, sister and stepmother. My dad's youngest sister died at forty two, as mentioned previously. His father at sixty seven, when at the IRS office, his name was called out, he stood up and died! My father's eldest sister at sixty three, then finally himself at sixty two. His younger brother passed exactly one week before - one at twelve am and the other at twelve pm. Their lives were hard but all seemed to rise above the circumstances they were born unto for the most part.

We were ethnically Sicilian, with German-Irish and later to find out) a bit of American Indian.

My eldest sister married Irish...he died at thirty nine after years of suffering.

My second sister married Italian, and she makes him suffer. Surprisingly, he is not dead.

My youngest sister married a German, and he died at fifty two.

They all had two children each. All have suffered their own personal torment.

I began to work on my middle sister who suffered with Parkinson's disease. My heart ached for her and her children. I tried to do everything that I could to help her. I would pray and pray for answers, for a medicine man of sorts, someone who could bring something to the table that I wasn't able to or who would understand what was happening.

This would go on for some time, and I would exhaust myself trying to help her with my ability to transfer energy, so much so that when I would finish, I would nearly pass out. It would work for a while, squelching the tremors and give her mobility, but then return. I never gave up, no matter, and kept praying each day.

I received a gift from someone whom I held dear to me. It was a book written by a native healer, Medicine Grizzly Bear.

I read and read, and in its conclusion, his address and white name was included. I gathered my thoughts and began to pursue him, reaching out. Finally, the connection was made•. And this was to be another stop along the way.

I began talking to this gentleman on the phone, explaining the reasons why I contacted him. I told him of the three crows who came to visit me. Eventually I was able to meet him in person while he was traveling in my area. He was not what I had expected in appearance, but, never the less, felt that he had plenty to offer. We spoke at length. I listened to him speak of stories and the human condition, of trials and tribulations that he had experienced in his own life. I found him to be quite sincere regarding his beliefs, medicine, and philosophy. I stayed in touch with him from that day forward. I read two more books he authored. Could this be what I had prayed for? Would he be able to help my suffering sibling or share something with me so that I could?

His first impression of me, after we spoke, was that I was a "diamond in the rough," and that I had what he referred to as "bear medicine" I told him of my experiences with the bears, the animals, and my other relations in nature. After much consideration and thought, at my own expense, I contacted him and made arrangements to have him come to my family's home and do what he would call "doctor" my sister with the Parkinson's.

During that visit he would also share the building and ceremony of the sweat lodge, which is an ancient ritual found in many cultures around the world, but in this case, pertaining to the spirituality of many of the indigenous peoples of the Americas. This was appropriately so - a ceremony that was performed by the Lenape people here, where I was born and raised. Preparations were being made for the upcoming week with this gentleman, each other, and the natural world.

We set out for my mother's home where my sister resided with her husband and two children. The home was located on what was called the "Irish lot." The street was named for its Revolutionary War resident, and he and his sister's graves were still located on that street. There were rumors of unmarked slave graves and Lenape burial grounds as well. The home, in its inception, was troubled to say the least, and sat partially finished for many years due to unexpected tragedies of those whom were having it built. I was told that someone was bitten by a black widow spider as it sat there as just a foundation and stairs. There was an underground stream that ran beneath it. Spirits were seen there over the years by myself, siblings, and their children.

As the ceremony and healing was commencing, my sister, who had seemed to be excited about the concept initially, became more and more nervous, shaking and babbling. The man continued to pray, smudge, and sing in his native language. I could see he was having difficulties. His regalia broke into pieces as he tried to put it on. The tools of his medicine went missing while his apprentice and I smudged the lower level of the home with pepperwood. My sister began freaking out. Suddenly, the man stopped. He was obviously troubled, and without words took his things and left the home, refusing to re-enter.

I saw my sister in a different way that day, a way that I found to be disturbing as he. I would never feel the same way about her again, and in time, would learn that she was suffering for a reason. Inside her she held all of the sins, I believe, of her forebears. The dead would speak to her often. Her selfishness, her lies and deceitful actions before and after this incident would come to light for all to see. She continued to live in her personal hell, drove away her siblings from her life, imprison her children with guilt and promises of gifts, something she had been doing for some time, hut at the cost of her family, including our mother.

This was clarity for me. The cycle must be stopped if we ever want to be free. We are not who our families are - we are who our spirits are. We don't always appear on the outside what we are on the inside. Even though we may share blood and parents, it doesn't mean that we are the same, or that we have an obligation to be the same. From this very moment, my way forward was to be my own. I continued to help my siblings and their children with new energy to change the path ahead. In some instances there was success, but in others, failure. The repercussions of their lack of attention to what I spoke of still lingers on, one difficulty after the next, and continues for their children as well.

Another case involved my youngest of three sisters. She had lost her husband just days before Christmas. Their relationship had been struggling, and now with the loss her struggle deepened. She had two children, both girls. Her life with her husband had been difficult. Not financially, but emotionally and spiritually. She would never really know him until long after he passed. She began going through his things, finding out about the man he had kept hidden, the man he suppressed. This man also bore many of the burdens of growing up in a less than stellar home. Though affluence and opportunity were not what it lacked, it did, however, lack honesty, warmth, and a sense of family. From the eyes of the onlooker it would all seem to be right, showy, proper and dignified as one might expect from a family from such a prestigious area.

My sister continued to deal with the anger that had overcome her like a plague. This anger carried over to all aspects of her life and towards all that had previously been involved with her and her husband for so many years before. Her children suffered in silence, trying to cope with the loss of their father, the anger of their mother and their own personal struggles that would, someday, come to light for one and still baffle another.

Jumping ahead, my sister was having trouble breathing. I already had many sessions of counsel with her in regards her anger and frustration. She was seeking treatment or minimally an answer to what was troubling her physically. I treated her in the past while she was dealing with night sweats, restlessness, and poor circulation in her feet (which was so bad that she was warned that if she didn't stop smoking the chances were they would be removed in the future). The night sweats and sleeplessness may have been as simple as menopause, and I recommended that she take Black Cohosh for the sleep issue, which is a supplement that contains tryptophan, the chemical found in turkeys that makes you feel sleepy. The poor circulation to her feet was resolved by using cayenne pepper sprinkled into her socks and worn to bed, also mixing a bit with a carrier oil and massaging it into the feet. All seemed to be improving, I also helped her with some unresolved back issues.

The answers she was getting for her breathing were a bit sketchy. No one would commit to a particular cause. She was told that she had COPD and began treatment for it - but did not feel any better.

She came over for an energy healing with me. All went as normal. My hands were on her back, over her heart and between her lungs. She started to become extremely uncomfortable. She said that as I kept my hands there it felt like needles were running through that part of her body. I felt something strange as well, and it gave me a feeling of sadness to boot. I knew it wasn't COPD. What I thought and felt I didn't want to share with her at that time. I recommended her to return to her doctor, or maybe find another for more x-rays and tests.

A couple of days before Christmas, my sister had an appointment with a pulmonary specialist. He took over her case from another doctor. When he reviewed her x-rays, he asked her to come in. I went along and my eldest sister as well. We sat there together in the examining room. Then, with tears in his eyes and a cracked voice he said, "I'm sorry you have a growth between your lungs and a mass in your lower lobe. It's cancer, small cell lung cancer." He was so upset that I was upset for him. My sister asked, "How long?" He replied, "Eleven weeks without treatment." She stayed strong but shocked. I looked at her, and trying to break the tension yelled out, "We are MexiCANS, not

MexiCAN'TS. We will beat this." Of course, we are not Mexican at all but I always wanted to use that phrase! (Thank you, George Lopez)!

The treatment was about to take a different turn. It would be approached in a ceremonial setting with all the pieces in place. I contacted my native friend and explained to him what my intentions were. I asked his permission, out of respect and protocol, to use one of his ceremonies - one that he called a pegasoy. This is a type of confession or atonement ceremony to clean the mind and spirit of past indiscretions and violations against natural law whether by your own hand or something carried over from your forebears, spouse, etc. He wished me luck. The area was prepared for her arrival - smudged, prayed over and cleansed. It would also require the energy and prayers of four additional people, each representing one of the four powers of creation and directional spirits. There were certain protocol to be followed involving this particular ceremony, but I am not obliged to share, for they are not mine to do so. As I awaited the arrival of the other four participants and my sister, I was outside making prayers to the creator and nature. There were a small flock of sparrows in a bush near my home. As I prayed for strength and cleansing, a sparrow hawk came out of the sky, flew just a couple of feet above the ground and directly into the bush where the birds were. There was a little scuffle, but no birds flew away. The sparrow is a very strong bird with incredible ability to survive and adapt any place under any conditions. The chirping stopped - the hawk left.

It was time, and momentarily all involved arrived. We set ourselves up in a circle, with my sister at the center and prayed, sending good and healing energy to her and for her. I began to work on her first. After her pegasoy, and using energy from my hands, I gathered the sickness from her body and concentrated it into one place. Then using humming bird medicine, I sucked the sickness out and spit it into a fire. Next, my Chilean friend and spiritual woman, knelt over her praying in her native language, also gathering sickness and pushing it away from her. Her voice was calming as the sea, and in a hypnotic cadence, tears ran down her face as she prayed and did her work. It was a very intense and emotional sight to behold. As I looked at the others in the circle, they also wept as they prayed but stayed focused on the task for which they came. Not too long after this ceremony, my sister went for all of the necessary testing that she would need to begin her planned treatment. With great surprise, due to the type of cancer that she was inflicted with, the doctor stated that all of the cancer was contained in one area. A growth resembling fingers wrapped around the area between the lungs, with just trace amounts in the lower lobe of one lung. This almost never happens as this form of cancer is, for the most part, a death sentence. Her treatment commenced. Six years have passed, and she is still alive, well and cancer-free. She does, however, suffer with residual damage from radiation.

She has received a second chance to live life. She thanks her doctors and staff at the cancer center regularly, but in conversation, even with those doctors, she thanks that day and the days previously spent with me and my people for saving her life.

The bond with nature and the spirits continued to grow stronger. I would participate and then commence many sweat lodge ceremonies for mental, physical and spiritual purification and growth. I would work on many more people, all with different types of issues. This, too, became a way of life for me going forward. The closer and more bonded I became with the natural world, the stronger the medicine grew. I was asked by many to just pray for them or to sit and have counsel with them or to help them learn and understand themselves or their circumstances. During the days to come many things would occur that removed doubt out of what was happening.

One day, through conversation with a group of acquaintances, I met a young lady who seemed to be of very good heart and spirit. We began talking and after a while being in her company, I got to know her. She had been trying to conceive for a very long time and was unsuccessful. At some point in her earlier life, she had an illness that threw her entire body out of balance. She was once a slim, beautiful, semi-professional singer with long thick hair and a face to die for. Her voice, in those younger years, was crisp and vibrant. Now it seemed that this couldn't have been possible. Her voice, frail and crackly, her body one of an older woman who had gone through her childbearing years, her hormones out of balance and showing it.

She was constantly saddened by her childless state. She was stepmother to two girls and loved them both very much, but had to battle for that love with their birth mother, even though her husband had custody. Eventually the birthmother would taint the girl's opinion of this woman. She separated her from these girls whom she had been with for quite some time, being loved and raised by her while their mom was off on her own. I sensed her feeling of emptiness, loss, and the deep sadness that ran through her being. She heard of what I did and represented and slowly opened up a bit more. Finally, she brought herself to ask if I could help her, and I agreed.

I worked on her in a ceremonial fashion at first, followed by prayer and energy healing and some counsel. We would do this twice. She said she felt good and a little more confident. She took my advice to forget about getting pregnant for now and go about her life as normal - but not to put any thought into it and to find things to keep her busy, happy and healthy. We would speak occasionally after that, and she would say that she was doing what I had suggested. She came to the realization that some things just may never be.

A couple of months later, while I was traveling for work, I received a call very early in the morning. It was her, and she was filled with excitement. She told me she was pregnant. She couldn't believe it and thanked me for it. I was so happy for her, and in some sense, couldn't believe it either.

A month went by, and we spoke again. She told that she had lost the baby and was very down. I consoled her and let her know that this was meant to be. For now she knew she would be able to conceive again. Her body wasn't healthy enough to carry yet, but was on the right track. Not too much later, she gave birth to a beautiful and healthy daughter. Her life at home would become what she always wanted. Her health returned, and all the love she had to give was as strong as ever.

I would go through something similar with another woman, one I love so dearly. She would give me the family that I had dreamed of in my earliest plans as a boy, perhaps not in the way that I had planned, but nonetheless what I needed and desired to make me a whole person. I found myself speaking to and praying for three additional women - one a relation of my daughter-in- law; one a friend of hers; and another a new neighbor of mine. I prayed for them for an extended amount of time and had conversations with them from time-to-time. They all conceived, when it seemed that it wasn't going to happen. Two of them were taking treatment for female issues that prevented them from conceiving, and the third was about to go on fertility drugs. My heart tells me that the prayers for them were heard and answered. The natural world brought to them the greatest gift they could ever receive. This would be just another stop along the way.

MY RELATIONS IN NATURE

MOM AND CUB

RED TAIL

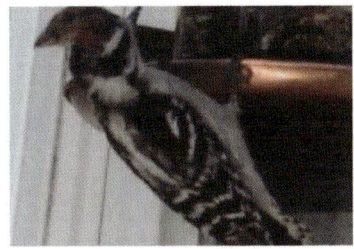

FLICKER BIRD

FAWN

GIANT WOODPECKER

BEAR AT MY DOOR

RAVEN

BIRTHDAY GUEST

My job as a trucker had, and would continue, to take me out into America and Canada. Along the way I would be in a constant state of awareness of all that surrounded me, all that was alive.
My relations in nature would accompany me on all my journeys, and their presence in my life brought me peace and comfort. I felt the connection grow stronger each day. Red tail hawks rode with me and let me know their presence. They are spiritual guardians and can bring messages from the natural worlds if you listen. There are many examples of our bond together but I will only mention a couple.

One day, while my truck was broke down in New England, I sat in a parking lot waiting for a service person to arrive. The wait grew long, and the day was wasting. I began to think in a spiritual way, asking natures spirits for some help. In the corner of my eye I saw a hawk flying overhead. I called out to him in his language. He came closer and began flying in circles over my truck. I could sense he was trying to help by bringing me a message. He came down from the sky. We whistled to each other as he flew closer. He broke his pattern of circles and flew towards the entrance of the place where I was parked and then came back. He made a few more circles, whistled, and flew off. This compelled me to exit my vehicle. Walking around to the front of it (mind you, this was a large, empty, paved and cleaned parking lot) I heard him talk again. Looking down onto the ground, I saw a quartz crystal and picked it up. As I glanced towards the sky, the hawk circled once more and then flew towards the mountains. The crystal was natural quartz with a reddish tint. Looking at it, I realized it was in the shape of a perched hawk with red tinted tail feathers. At that very moment, I knew that this was a gift from the hawk, and I tried to thank him. As I looked back down, the service truck that I had been waiting for arrived from the entrance that the hawk had flown to. First came the ravens and crows, then came the hawks. Both would stay with me and continue to do so. They would come to visit me no matter where I was. While I was on the road, the ravens and the crows would leave me gifts of one feather at a time. How do I know they were gifts? I would exit my truck to deliver goods to a facility. When I returned to my truck, a feather would be next to it, right beside the driver door, and it hadn't been there previously. This didn't happen once, but six or seven times over the course of a few years. The hawks would fly over the top of the truck, so close that I could look up and almost be able to touch them. Sometimes

RED TAIL HAWK

they would fly directly next to me, and I would roll down the passenger window to talk with them as we ran down the highway. They, too, left gifts of feathers. Where I am they are - and we are one. I thank them always for visiting with me and for sharing their medicine. They speak to my spirit, as do the crows and ravens, and I speak with theirs. My bond with the natural world grew undisputable.

The bears were also a connection that I made previously. As my personal spirituality grew, so did our relationship. On numerous occasions along the way, I would have more time with the bears as they would come to my home more often. We communicated, respected, and trusted each other. They also began to appear and show themselves to those for whom I prayed. The bear was another messenger from nature. I tried very hard to listen each time we were together. On three or more occasions, we were within a few feet of each other. I walked along with them and spoke to them in words and sang a bear song; we both hadn't any fear. Our chats seemed quite natural - a man and his bear friend. The bears first came to me when I prayed to their spirits, and the spirits of nature, to come and visit me at my home. They did when I was in the company of my daughter-in-law and her little cub. They, too, would establish a relationship with a bear that visited at their home, a relationship of respect and admiration. Each time the bear visits them it is a sign of protection and strength and of the bond that was made that day. The bear visits all who hold a part of my heart. He comes in a good way, and they can talk to him without fear. He has even obliged when being asked for permission to photograph him, as in the case of a very dear friend of mine whom I love and care for very much. She was at my home with my partner when the bear came to visit. My partner spotted him at the front door. My friend's first reaction was to walk outside and ask the bear for a photo so she could send it to me, and he agreed. She took a few more pictures of him while he was standing just feet away from her. She didn't fear him - she knew him as a spirit and a messenger. Knowing that I had been waiting for him to visit, she was sad that I was not at home when he appeared. Never the less, that particular visit may not have been for me. Two weeks later, while outside of my home, a big mommy bear and her yearling cub came to visit with me. I was elated by their visit! She stopped walking, and we spoke a little. Coming up behind her was her beautiful cub. I greeted and welcomed them. While they

BIG MALE BEAR AT THE DOOR

MOM AND CUB STOPPING BY

lumbered along, I walked behind them and watched them play and wrestle in the grass. It was a blessing to behold!

Along the way, I continued to pray. I stood under the stars before leaving my home with some tobacco. Tobacco, in some American Indian beliefs, is the most sacred of plants. One of the creation stories of the Ojibwa tells that when the creator was making the earth and it was ready for planting, he threw a handful of seeds upon it. Tobacco was the first of the plants to grow. If you wanted to speak to the creator or other spirits, you would offer them tobacco before beginning. Following this story, that is how I began. As I have learned in time, the circle is life, and all things are in the circle. I began my prayers by giving thanks to the creator for life, then Mother Earth for all her gifts, and thanks for the blessings of food, shelter and clothing; to the four powers of creation, the four directions (each representing a certain power and purpose: starting by facing east, turning right to the south, then west, north, and back to the east, creating a circle with myself in the center); to the sky, who watches over us; to the spirits, and to my relations in nature. These prayers expanded as I traveled further down my spiritual path.

In the beginning I prayed for safe passage on my journey and for peace and balance in mind, body and spirit - and made prayers for those that I loved. In the evening, I would pray for the completion of the day, for good dreams, and, again, for those that I loved. This became part of my life going forward. No matter where I was or whom I was with, the day started and ended with prayer. As I encountered more people on my journey, I was requested to make healing prayers for them. I wasn't sure that I was the person they needed to pray for them, but they seemed to think so, and I honored the requests. At some point, it was taking forty five minutes or more to mention the people who asked for prayers for their issues, beside my own personal prayers. The more I prayed, I felt the connection grew stronger and that my prayers were truly being heard. In many different ways, they also were being answered. The answers did not come from a voice in the heavens or from angels. They were answered by the visits of different birds, animals, or insects which would represent a feeling, circumstance, a physical property, or a message of hope, strength and reflection. As mentioned earlier, when praying and working on people close to me, a bear would show up in their lives. A hawk would appear to them on their journeys. A raven or crow would make themselves apparent to those who needed their medicine. For a beloved friend of mine, it was a cardinal. One day, while eating my dinner, something flew into my window and made a loud bang. I looked up and saw what appeared to be a blood stain on the window, but no victim. On further investigation, the blood stain was not blood at all, but little, tiny red feathers. I ran outside to see what had bit the window and to make sure it was okay. There was nothing on the ground, but I heard some chirping from a tree nearby. I saw a male cardinal and asked him if he was the one who had hit the window. He began shaking his head and chirping as if to answer me "yes." I asked him, 'Were you trying to get my attention?" He answered in the same manner once again. I walked back into my home and sat down. Immediately I felt, in my spirit, that he had come to let me know that my dear friend needed me. I called her home, and asked "What is wrong?" She replied, in a whisper of a voice, "How did you know to call? Things are not very good here right now -having a lot of trouble with my husband." I told her that the cardinal had come to me to let me know that something was wrong by how he went about getting my attention by practically knocking himself out on my window. I offered her sanctuary if she needed it, but she declined. After the death of her grandmother, whom she loved very much, cardinals began to make appearances in her life. She mentioned this to another relative who told her that her deceased grandmother had loved cardinals. The cardinals have been with her since. Any time I see or encounter one of these beautiful birds and it goes out of its way to get my attention, I know to immediately contact my friend and check on her and her well-being.

Once, on a summer morning, I was in an area of New England that was very familiar to me, having traveled this road for many years. I found it quite beautiful. It was rural with a nostalgic feel - country stores, farms and large open spaces. I came upon an intersection, a cross roads, with nothing but open land on all four corners. As the light turned green, I began to accelerate and shifted gears, one after another. While appreciating the ambiance and beauty of this place, a small bird flew by my windshield. It was very close and startled me. I wasn't able to react quickly and stop the truck. The bird was very pretty and looked as if it had come from the sun with wings that looked like fire. It made it past my truck, and I felt relieved that I hadn't hit it. Suddenly, it turned, as if to try to fly into my open window. I moved further back into my seat to let it in without hitting me, but it didn't make it inside. I am not sure what happened, but it might have been caught in a back draft and hit the mirror of my truck. I felt upset and worried that it had been killed or, perhaps, injured, and was lying on the road only to be run over by another passing vehicle. Frantically, I kept looking into my rearview mirrors trying to see the ground behind me and looked around to the front windshield to make sure it wasn't trapped, but I couldn't see it. Continuing to drive at a slow pace through the crossroads, I spotted a big raven at the edge of the road. He was bouncing up and down, then pecking the ground with its beak. As I drove closer, I could hear it squawking. Instantly I knew that the raven was trying to tell me something. My first thought was that he was pissed off and was scolding me because he saw me hit the unidentified bird, and not stop to look for it. He kept up his dance, inching closer to the road, his squawks growing louder. Was he laughing at me? At this point I was getting freaked out and began to feel that this had been a test from the spirits and that I had failed. Just as I thought everything was going well in my life as a spiritual person, was I now going to have to pay for my negligence? I drove past the raven, and he looked at me and went silent but continued to jump up and down. Suddenly, I felt something sticking me in the back, under my shirt, between myself and the truck seat. I reached back to feel for a twig or a bee, or maybe one of my necklaces had come undone, but found nothing. A little further down the road, I felt the same poking, but this time it was lower. Pulling over to the side of the road, I set the air brake and moved the seat forward as close to the steering wheel as I could. I reached behind myself and felt something there and, fearfully, pulled it out. "Holy Shit," I screamed. It was a bird, not just any old bird, but the most beautiful bird I had ever seen. It was the very same bird who flew past my windshield, the same bird who hit my mirror and disappeared. He seemed stunned but quite alive.

Putting him in the passenger seat, we took off! Along the way, I spoke to him. I apologized for hitting him and reassured him that it was not my intention. After taking a few pictures of him with my cell phone, I sent them off to my niece in Maine, who was studying to be a naturalist. She identified the bird as a Baltimore oriole. 'Wow, far from home, aren't you?" I thought. We drove for miles together. I picked him up and put him on my belly to comfort and pet him. From there he went onto my dashboard, and then jumped onto my finger like a domestic bird. Finally, he

BALTIMORE ORIOLE

SAYING GOODBYE

found his perch upon the steering wheel. He stayed there for the next thirty minutes. As I would turn it, he remained steadfast and turned with it! Crazy! Finally, I reached my destination.
Before departing the truck, I opened the passenger window for him. I said, "Thank you for the visit, and I hope you find your way home!" He didn't move but was free to do so. I made my delivery which took about twenty minutes. Returning to the truck, I found that he was still sitting in the passenger window. "Why are you still here?" I asked. "Do you want to tell me something?" He turned and looked toward me, then looked out the window as if to say goodbye or thank you. He looked once more and then flew out the window. Once my trip was over, I researched the Baltimore oriole and looked for what it represented to me in a spiritual way. It represented the power of the sun, a loner bird, with a beautiful song, but not common in New England. He was a spirit and one with a message. The raven wanted me to know that. Since then, a Baltimore oriole comes to visit me at my home every summer. It lets its presence be known and fly's away, only to return again the following summer. This is a medicine bird for me, He shares his power and purpose and his message is clear. He is mentioned in my prayers each day.

Along the way, my relationship to the natural world became part of my everyday life. I looked forward to seeing my hawks, ravens, Baltimore orioles, my friends the deer, the bears, raccoons, songbirds, and eventually eagles, giant woodpeckers and flicker birds. On more than one occasion, as I would be saying my outdoor prayers in the middle of the night with my eyes cast towards the sky, I would feel something nearby. It sometimes felt as if it were standing behind me. I would try to overcome my fear of what I couldn't see by standing tall and not allowing my prayers to be interrupted. Often, the volume of my speech would increase as a way of blocking out what I was hearing and feeling in the dark. One time, as I stood as usual, the sounds of movement in the dark night were growing closer and closer to me. I continued to pray louder and harder, as whatever was out there approached. I felt the hair on the back of my neck stand up. As my muscles tightened, I put myself into a defense mode, preparing for something I was unsure of. Reaching into my pocket, I pulled out my lighter and continued to pray. I felt a presence close behind me in the pitch black of night. Deciding to use the element of surprise and a loud voice to scare whatever happened to be there, I lit my lighter and spun around like a Ninja. I held the lighter as if it were a lantern trying to illuminate the snow covered ground. As I looked np and my eyes focused BAM, there it was! The white ghostly face of a very large female deer. "What's doing?" I asked. "I'm glad it's only you. You scared the shit outta me!" She stood there in the glow of my lighter, looking almost angelic, calm, poised and unafraid. I bid her goodbye and walked past her to my car. She watched as I departed my driveway.

My encounters with deer would continue to be one of peace. They came in herds to my home. When preparing for a sweat lodge, they would come and stand off to the sides of my property. They took comfort in my presence and also in the presence of my spiritual sisters next door. They, too, became as one with them as they fed and nurtured the loners, battle scarred and sickly. At home during the weekend, I would stand near my sweat lodge and pray near the fire pit. In the morning light, the deer would come to watch. One female stood close to me as I prayed. Sometimes I would bring her food. One particular morning, she saw me and came over while I was praying. She sniffed the air and let me know that she was looking for food. Glancing up at her, I noticed she was standing a few feet from me in a circle of stones that I had placed on the ground around some shrubs. I told her, under no uncertain terms that if she wanted to eat, should would have to stay for the prayers. And stay she did, inside her very own prayer circle with her head bowed, until the praying was done. She would come back from time to time to join me in the circle.

These experiences are very sacred to me. They speak volume's, in a spiritual aspect, of being connected to the natural world, as one with all things. I have always treated animals, birds, and plants with the same passion and love that I would treat a human who needed my kind of help. Whether it be an injured bird, squirrel, deer or domestic pet, I worked on them all in the same manner.

One evening, while driving home on a dark, rural road next to a place called Bear Pond, my partner yelled, "I think you just passed a baby deer. It looks like it's been hit. You have to stop, you have to help it." I pulled over, and walked back in the dark to see what happened. There was a tiny fawn lying on the ground.

It had been hit by car and appeared to be unconscious, but not broken. I saw down with her on the side of the road, next to the shoulder. She was unresponsive. I began to pray and offer tobacco. Putting my hands on its head and body, I began to use energy medicine. She remained still and in shock. As I worked on the fawn, I began singing, in a sacred way, a deer song, and one that until that moment I had not known. Holding its head in my hands, I blew energy into its forehead, using my mouth. In my mind I visualized the energy flowing and continued to do this about three or four times, and then stop. Happily, the little fawn started shaking its head, a little at first, and then more and more. With its eyes opened wide, it continued to rest. I asked if it knew where its momma was, telling it that I was sure she was close by. Helping it to its feet and gaining its balance, I pet it for a short time to give it comfort and continued speaking to it. Giving her a little kiss on the head and a couple of pats on her butt, I told her to go to her momma. Off she went into the woods. I returned to my car. My partner was laughing and said, "Who is going to believe this like it's normal or common to stop and do a healing on a baby deer in the middle of the road, like it's no big deal!

After the building of the sweat lodge in my backyard, groups of people came to attend ceremonies to pray, seek wisdom and knowledge, cleansing and peace. The vibration level of the surrounding increased and felt and appeared to be much more than some grass, trees and rocks. It became, through the eyes of those who came to visit, a sanctuary or sacred ground. The animals and birds made their presence known each day, coming in numbers and varieties, also staying to find peace and comfort.

One summer, I decided to hold a few sweat lodge ceremonies over the course of a weekend. While waiting for those who were participating to gather at my home, I stood on my deck having a conversation with the Native American gentleman who would be giving the lecturing and conducting the ceremonies. Also present was an old friend of his, and a new friend of mind. His friend studied for an extended amount of years with native healers, medicine women, and also traditional college, earning a degree as a psychotherapist. We talked, and the day was absolutely beautiful. The deck overlooked the lodge, and to the rear was a small wooded area and a stone knee wall. All was green and plush. The gentlemen and his friend had been at my home and sweat lodge before, and both had instructed myself and my

BABY DEER

people in the construction of the lodge and shared protocol, prayer and procedures, but not in great detail. They felt that sharing sacred and indigenous traditions might sully or dilute the beliefs of their people. Previously, I shared many of the stories of my life with him, many concerning my animal experiences, especially the bears. He was very strict in his teaching and beliefs. He believed that there was a certain way that one would or could be chosen to lead a spiritual person's life. In order to learn his way and bond from all things in the universe would take years of training and following certain ancient ways, rituals and having certain experiences. His beliefs would, on some level, make me doubt all that had happened to me and make it seem that it was all my imagination or simple coincidence. This bothered me deeply and felt somewhat insulting. Meditating through prayer, I asked that something happen during his visit here to change his thoughts towards me, and compel him to share more with me. I wanted some respect for what I had already gone through, long before I was aware of him and sought his guidance.   Suddenly, he began to sing in a very soft voice, staring towards the wooded area. He called to me to look. My eyes tried to follow where he was focused. There it was, the proof, the acknowledgement - my brother, the bear! He walked from the trees into my yard and headed directly towards the sweat lodge. He stopped at the fire pit, just outside of it. He walked right to the entrance as if he were going to enter. At that moment, my longtime K-9 companion noticed that we were all looking at something and left the deck to protect her ground. I called her back and she barked a little, but did not run to or near the bear.

This was shocking because she didn't allow many outsider animals on her land. The bear turned calmly and walked to the trees. It was hesitant as it walked, hesitant to leave. It stood up, took a look once again at the lodge and at us, then left. My native friend smiled and was illuminated. He said, "There you go. He has brought his blessings, and this is now a bear lodge" (meaning that the bear would be the medicine). I looked at my friend and said, "I am so happy that my relations came to visit while you were here, for now you know!" Later that evening, we had our lodge and many attended. The bear visit was mentioned and explained to those unaware of its significance and importance.

My native friend would treat me differently from that day forward and would refer to me as "Bear Man".

sweat lodge frame

THE EAGLES

Along the way everything had made sense. All things were coming together. The dots were connecting. Relationships with the spiritual and natural worlds were being strengthened each day.

The animals and birds were making regular appearances to my home and to the lives of those who came to seek some help or guidance. The giant woodpeckers started to come and visit. The flicker birds, their smaller relatives, took up residence at my home. Gold finches, cardinals, chickadees and the orioles, who would come for their yearly visits. Different species of hawks, blue herons, and all types of beautiful song birds.

The animals and the birds came during and after prayers. They brought messages with them that would relate to the particular concerns that were being prayed about, or for the person being prayed for. Those closest to me would also experience an unusual relationship with nature, in person and in dreams, helping them to find answers or a direction to go that they may have been seeking.

We conducted ourselves like a small village and shared the everyday burdens together. We prayed together, we sweat together, laughed and cried together. We would reach out to help those that we could and always our relations in nature.

Life for me was peaceful and fulfilling. With this came clarity. All of the plans of my youth, as far as the things I had wanted for myself, had come to fruition. I found myself surrounded by women, once again, as in my early days. This time, however, it was my turn to help them, to care for them as the old Sicilian women cared for me as a baby.

Their lessons, though at the time I had no idea, would be invaluable. They instilled and influenced my life more than I could have known. In retrospect, they must have known, or been able to sense, what was ahead for me. They prepared a strong foundation with the values they had planted. My life going forward would reflect these values. I would, in some ways, become a little more ethnic as I grew older, in regards to traditions, cuisine, and the use of their language. To quote from The Karate Kid, "The key to a strong banzai is a strong root." All of the lessons that I had learned, from these women, my father, my mother, the soldiers, and other male and female relatives and acquaintances in my life were now crystal clear. It all made great sense! There was only one way to go, and that way was forward.

The hard lessons of the past would not be dwelled upon but put into context and stored within my spirit to be drawn upon when needed and to help me get perspective, when helping another who may have been going through a similar circumstance. This is My medicine.

Our time on earth and the things that we encounter, experience and endure, are what makes us who we become. We can either use these lessons as a source of strength and wisdom, or succumb to the negative cause and effects they may represent. Allowing them to linger and fester in our spirits will eventually affect our minds and bodies. It's a long and difficult road of self-examination, taking a great deal of effort and energy. On the other hand, to allow these experiences to keep one mired in the swamp of struggle and hard times, would be unconscionable, taking the same amount of effort and energy, but going nowhere.

Each of us has a story, a struggle, whether personal or shared thru relations or close friends. We shouldn't suffer along with another why they fight their battle and not take the time to realize that it is not our battle to fight. Our battles will come, and we will need to be strong to persevere. Love and support for those who are fighting is a good thing. Prayers and laughter alike heal. All individuals, we need to remain strong for ourselves. When those we love and those we care for come to their crescendo, their final performance, we will still be there to fight another day. This was the most difficult lesson for me and will be for many.

With all the good and solid things that were happening along the way on my journey of purpose, there was still something missing.

The Indian peoples have always held the Eagle in the highest regard. They say it was the only bird that could fly high enough to take your prayers to the creator. It was an honor and spiritual benchmark to have a bond with this sacred creature. The medicine people, chiefs, and warriors would receive the gift of an Eagle feather marking certain accomplishments within their lives.

I won't go into any details or translate on these pages what they might be for it is not my place nor my culture to comment on. That being said, I do have a great respect for their wisdom, philosophy, medicine and their knowledge of the natural world, including their spiritual beliefs. In my opinion, they are the closest to the earth. They feel and hear her heartbeat and her pain and sickness. They love and honor her. In the past, and in some areas today, indigenous cultures live as one with her.

As I mentioned previously, I felt a profound connection to these people and a very spiritual connection to the Lenape and Lenapehoking (their land). With all the heart and soul that I had been putting into my spiritual journey, where were the eagles?
Why aren't they visiting me? The best I could come up with was that they didn't show because I wasn't ready, because I didn't hit that benchmark or milestone. Even though I am not an Indian shouldn't laws of the natural world still apply? The spirits and the ancestors would determine when and if that would become my reality. It wasn't something that was going to happen because I wanted it to or thought that it should. I spent many days looking to the skies over the New England mountains and in my heart and spirit talked to the universe and the spirit of the eagle. "I mention you in my prayers every day. Am I doing something wrong?" This went on for some time.

I cannot remember the course of events or circumstances which would unfold along the way. I kept mentioning and thanking them in my prayers and not give their appearance another thought. Then, it happened...on the road, in the early part of the day, coming out of the sun, I was compelled to look towards the mountains. I saw something in the glare of the sun, and it came closer. I looked in the mirrors of my truck and found myself, temporarily, alone. Suddenly, it came out to the highway just at the edge of the trees, maybe fifteen feet above my truck.
My first eagle!!! My skin filled with goose bumps, and I could feel the power and significance of this majestic bird. It made a couple of circles. I could see it clearly. It flew back towards the sun and the mountains. This was a sight to behold! I prayed and offered its spirit tobacco to thank it for its visit. At the time I was not sure if this was coincidence but wasn't thinking so. I would have three more encounters with the eagle while on the road. All would happen in the same year and under similar circumstances.

My second encounter would take place high in the mountains of New England on a snowy day. Once again, finding myself alone again on the road, I spotted something in tree. Not being sure of what it was, I wasn't going to pay it any mind when it began moving and flapping its wings. I realized what it was an eagle! I greeted and spoke to it ,asking it not to fly away. It must have been waiting there for me, I thought. It began to take off, and I was just about to say goodbye when he turned towards my truck. He kept coming, getting lower in the air the closer he got. He made a quick turn and flew across the view from my windshield. I looked him directly in the eye and was beside myself. He flew up the road a couple of yards and perched on a low branch. As I drove by, he stayed there. I waved and thanked him. When the truck completely passed him, it flew off to the mountains.

My third encounter happened on the road as well, this time in a rural section of suburban Pennsylvania. Once again, finding myself temporarily alone on a busy highway, traveling about sixty miles an hour, just ahead of me I saw something in the road. The closer I came I could see that it made a kill of some sort or was eating road kill. It's back faced me, and I assumed it was a vulture. They are a common sight along the roads in the Northeast. As I got closer, it still wasn't moving, trying to fly, or jump out of the way. Vulture or not, I wasn't about to hit it with my truck. I started braking immediately almost coming to a complete stop. I began to lose sight of it over the hood of my truck. Then, it took flight right up over the hood. This was not a vulture at all - it was the third bald eagle, so close again that I could count the feathers of its underbelly! Immense in size, his wing span was almost as wide as the truck itself. I stopped in amazement. The eagle flew off, and down the road I went almost not sure that this had occurred.

These three encounters or visits were not in places where eagles were commonly seen.

Then, there was a fourth.on a back country road near a swamp that lie in front of some woods that led to a reservoir. This, I learned, was a common ground for eagles. As usual, I was alone on the road when I saw it. It flew from a tree to the swampy water and then back into the trees. What stood out was that I hadn't seen an eagle that looked like this before - this was spotted! Having read about spotted eagles in American Indian stories, I didn't know that they existed here. It was incredibly huge and beautiful with some of the most interesting markings. After my trip ended, and I returned home, I did research on what I had seen. It was a spotted eagle, which was an American Indian description of a young bald eagle before maturity. I truly stuck in my mind, the markings, the color, the size -just amazing!

The way in which my eyes had seen this eagle was if I had seen a spirit. There was a feeling inside that I could not identify, a feeling that there was more to this encounter, then at the time, I could realize.

SPIRITUAL STRENGTHENING

All was well. I spent weekdays at my chosen profession. On weekends I would take time for appointments for those who were interested in what I did. Most came by recommendation from friends of family who had already experienced my medicine Those who chose to participate, for the most part, were having stress-related issues - fatigue, aches, pains, bad dreams, and in some cases, depression. Sessions began with conversation, allowing the person to open up and put out into the universe what it was they were seeking or from what problems they were suffering. From that point, I would make an assessment of whether I thought my medicine would be effective for them and their needs. I am not able to help everyone nor will I claim to. I can and do, however, help a great deal of folks in one way or another.

The practice of natural healing has many facets. I have found one that suits me well and that I feel confident in the use of prayer, healing energy (similar to the practice of Reiki) and the manipulation of that energy using my hands, in turn, allows a person to release their inner turmoil or demons. This assists them in obtaining new and clear thought, a better outlook for the future, and assists them in making sense of what has brought them to this place in their lives. In some cases the sessions would go on for an extended period of time. I tried everything that I could to help them open up their hearts, minds, and spirits to the natural world and to the notion that through the creator and universe any and all things are possible. Much time and energy was spent, often to the point of exhaustion. However, I did not feel that I was always effective. In cases where there was an emotional attachment to the individual, I would stay the course. Usually, under those circumstances, there had been much invested in their well-being, yet if I didn't feel that I made any real breakthrough (or at least, not in my opinion), I would back off. This allowed that person to digest what took place and experience the things we spoke of.

Everything isn't everything to everybody. As individuals, we process and digest things in our own ways. We have our own perceptions of what is what, and until we can identify that within ourselves, understanding ourselves and just how we fit into the web of life, it will be difficult to find peace and balance. For me personally, the journey of self-discovery, the finding of spirit came through, in some aspects, religion, but more based in nonpolitical spirituality - the spirituality of ancestors, prior to conquest , subjugation, and separation of man and God by organized religions.

I feel as though giving man the true freedom to worship the way that came naturally, and if spirituality belonged to the individual (not the church or some other man-made entity), this could be seen as dangerous to those whose agendas would prove throughout history to be that of control. This controlling would encompass not only the thoughts and hearts of people but also the gifts that the creator put here upon the soft and sacred earth for all whom inhabit it.

"Taking away their spiritual leaders, their culture, their language, their food and land. Make them be us. They should be grateful that we saved them from their existence. Ours is the right and only way. Now that they have forgotten who they are, we can control them" - these are MY words.

Speaking to the ancestors spirits, in indigenous people's beliefs, are a big part of their medicine and spirituality. The ancestors do not speak to all people but to those whom were chosen, groomed or trained as medicine people, visionaries, warriors and leaders. They assist them on their personal journeys and help them to guide their people as well. They are the old ones - they hold the wisdom, knowledge and power of time. These spirits have guided their people from the beginning. Some believe that these guardians came from elsewhere such as the stars. As an example, for the Hopi, the Kachinas are star people who came to show them how to survive, where to live, and in a way, gave them a set of commandments to live by. References to star people are found in many other indigenous people's beliefs.

As I would watch and listen to my own native friends making prayers and singing songs to the ancestors of their people, I could feel the connection they were making. I was able to sense something was there that I could not see with my own eyes but they could, some with earthly vision, and others, in what is called a sacred way. This was similar to the way that any devout person would pray to their deity yet different. In this case it would appear that whom they were praying to was standing before them. The prayers were a conversation between two worlds at its nexus. This was extremely powerful to observe while listening to songs and drumming of their people. The steady rhythms, the heartbeat of mother earth and their voices seemed to come directly from their spirits, carrying with it all of the voices of their predecessors. Closing my eyes allowed me to set my spirit free to hear and feel each word and bang of the drum.

Incorporating native music and rhythms into the healing work that I was doing on my own would prove to be beneficial. The music and rhythms made available to me were vast - some coming from recordings of traditional peoples, and others interpretations done in a very honorable way. I was particular about the ones that I chose, they had to speak to me and my spirit. The music, songs, prayers and stories, though I may not have understood them, allowed me to enter a different dimension a spirit world bringing me to focus and open my heart and mind and enabling me to be more in tune to the task at hand. It also allowed the person I was working on to join me in this realm. Some referred to this feeling as a shamanic trance. In my case these songs and rhythms allowed for a spiritual connection to happen between two beings and the universe they were part of. Along with the music were the scents and smells of ancient and sacred herbs. These herbs were placed on the earth in the beginning of time to help humans and animals alike. They are medicinal and are used in a variety of ways. My use for them included smudging's and offerings to the spirits. After adding a little bear root to be chewed, all of the senses would be stimulated creating the ambiance and tone for good healing - mentally, physically and spiritually.

My next stop along the way would be to solidify my relationship with the ancestors of the land where I was born. The people, who let their presence in my life be known at a young age, whom along with all of those who had shared wisdom and knowledge with me from the beginning, would also be doing the same. Their way, however, would be much more subtle and would have gone unnoticed to most, but as my journey of purpose unfolded, it became more apparent.

"The ancestors are here, and they are happy we are doing this ceremony. They are happy to hear these prayers and songs." As the night progressed and the last of the preparations were being made for a sweat lodge ceremony, these words rang out from native healer Medicine Grizzly Bear. Throughout these prayers, when a moment of silence surfaced, the trees rained acorns. Not just once, but at the end of each session. As the tone of the prayers and the energy of the ceremony accelerated, the raining of the acorns grew as well. The night came to its conclusion. In the morning I went out to the ceremonial ground to clean up. I noticed that my vegetable garden, which at the time was spent, had blossomed! There were new purple blooms on some of the plants. These plants hadn't produced anything for at least a month, yet in the morning sun, beautiful purple blooms! The blooms stayed on the plants for the duration, never producing fruit. Could this have been a visual thank you from the ancestors? Could this have been the response of the earth and all our relations in nature for hearing our prayers for them? Time continued and that memory would stay with me and all that attended that night. Are the spirit people here? Have they always been here? Is the fact that for possibly hundreds of years that have continued to live here in an alternate state of being, continuing to live their lives as they did during their times on this land?

The deer would come to my home as mentioned previously. On a wintery day there were a small herd of them in my backyard. A large picture window looked out over the area, creating a natural theater, a viewing box. The deer walked along the rock wall at the edge of the woods in single file - the same path that the bear walked later to give his blessings to our lodge. They, however, were walking in the opposite direction. They came upon a circle of rocks at the edge of my property. Here they stopped still in a single file formation. The first large female stood with her two front legs inside the shallow stone circle, her head bowed down. She stood there as a knight would at the moment of his coronation. From the window my partner snapped photos. We found that the way they were postured and their behavior was interesting and different from their usual pattern. After developing the film, which contained other subject matter, we began to go through them. To our surprise the photos of the deer showed more than what met the eye. There were orbs throughout the wooded area and streaks of light that were not visible at the time the photos were taken. The large female who stood in the circle with her head bowed had a full-figured spirit kneeling above it. Its hands were extended, looking as though petting the deer or giving it a blessing. Trying to be skeptical wasn't possible to me, it was extremely clear. I showed the photos to my Ciche (Mayan friend) and said nothing. His response was immediate. "That is a grandmother spirit holding something in front of her. That's beautiful." This was completely in sync with my assessment. The next stop for the photos was via e-mail to my native healer and spiritual man friend, Medicine Grizzly Bear. His response was, "Wow! I'm a little surprised that the spirits allowed you to take a picture of them. It's very unusual. They are reaching out to you and letting you know that they are with you. You are able to speak with them. They have been there and have always been there. Bond with them." And that's what I did. I was honored and knew in some way that they had been with me since the beginning. I suppose that all they had done in the past, in their subtle way, didn't close the deal in my non-Indian mind. There needed to be something I could see with my conscious eye. No more doubt, no more second guessing, time to learn. This was the next stop along the way.

THE ORBS

GRANDMOTHER SPIRIT

SPIRITS

The journey ahead was going to take a different direction. The connection and bonds with the spirit world of our ancestors would play an important role in my personal feeling of "I have arrived." Still praying each day, and now directing some of those prayers to the grandmothers and grandfathers of Lenapehoking, I spoke to them in my prayers the same way a child would speak to their grandparents. I asked those questions - who, what and why? I prayed for wisdom, knowledge and patience. Even though all of my life was spent on their lands, I began my journey to seek them. I attended numerous pow-wows trying to find remnants of their relations and pieces of their culture and continually read more about their traditions and culture. I began to teach myself a bit of their language translating part of the regimen of my prayers that I said each day into the Munsi (a band of Lenape) dialect in order to show my sincerity and respect, somehow knowing they were listening. Through my research I found out more and more - where they had their camps, the way they approached agriculture, and to me the most important, their spiritual beliefs and practices. The more I educated myself about these people, the more I realized that their influence had already taken place in my spiritual personality.

There were 500 nations' of Indian people in the United States prior to the invasion of the Europeans. They each had their own ways, customs and stories. All had spiritual beliefs that were personal to them, ceremonies, medicine, songs and dance. For me, as my interests and involvement and pursuit of knowledge went forward, the Lenape held closest to my way. I took more time, in those days, on a personal journey of growth. I put aside, for a while, the medicine that I had been practicing helping others, and use that time to fill my spirit. With the help of my dearest friend, the quest commenced.

We researched historical data available and maps and legends of the Lenape in the area that we lived and took time together to go to the places we had learned of. Some of these places were in our own backyards and others not too far away. We spent time out in the woods where we knew they had flourished. Once out of the sight of modern civilization we could feel their presence and understood why they called this place home. On those journeys we found the company of our relations in nature, listening to them and watching their behavior. We never viewed them as just being there, but more like tour guides. One experience that I will share in regards to the quest is, in my opinion, the most significant. While doing our research we came across some information pertaining to a large ceremonial ground and encampment where for possibly thousands of years the Lenape, in one form or another, had been gathering. They came to this place during certain parts of the year to pray and give thanks to the earth, all that it offered, to pray for their people, and the river that held their name. This river allowed all bands spread over three states to have a way and means to connect and to meet and gather at this sacred site.

One summer, when the time was right, off we went. We were not sure how we would achieve getting there for the land was in the middle of the river. Even with the aerial maps that were available to us we were not sure if we would be able to locate its entrance point. Starting on one side we made our way down to the water. The river was swollen and moving quite fast. Having only an inflatable boat and a couple of oars, we realized the chance of paddling across and landing where we wanted to, looked impossible. Contemplating how we would achieve what our mission without drifting long past our focus point left us clueless. We walked up and away from the river and back to the truck.

Approaching the truck we heard the crows talk. They were off in the distance, but their voices were clear. "Are you trying to tell us something?" I asked. They replied. "The crows called," I said to my friend. 'We should listen and follow their voice." So we did. We went back into the truck and took a short drive into the neighboring state, listening for the crows to guide us. When we found a place that felt right, I parked the truck. Nearby a fisherman was putting his gear away and as a courtesy, we gave greetings. He spoke to us of his time here fishing at the river which spanned many years. During the conversation, we found the opportunity to inquire about the island that we were seeking. He reached into his jacket and pulled out a map. "It sounds familiar, he said, "but I don't know of it the way you describe or by the name you call it. There is something like that across the street and through the woods. I was fishing there earlier." As we parted ways, we thanked him and walked towards the road. My eyes were drawn towards the ground, and there sat a crow or raven flight feather close to the road. It laid in a way that had appeared to be pointing to the river. Smiling, I picked up and turned to the man and my dear friend and said, "This is the way.

This the place. The crows have spoken." Their voices, now silent, had directed our way towards where we needed to be. Their gift of the feather was the sign that we had arrived.

We walked into the woods following the directions that the feather had pointed. A path in the woods ran parallel to the river. As we walked we remained quiet, listening to our hearts and nature. Coming upon the place that the fisherman described to us, we located an old boat launch. Not a boat launch in the conventional sense but a place where for many years canoers, kayakers, and sports fishermen used to gain entrance to the river. We continued down to the water's edge, carrying our inflatable boat and the crow feather, along with tobacco and sacred herbs. The plan was to go this sacred place with the intention of offering prayers to the river and to the spirits of those for whom in the past had done this themselves.

Finally reaching the water, we looked out across the river to chart our way to the place on the island where we could land and upon arriving traverse the banks - hopefully finding ourselves in the midst of the ceremonial ground.

As we looked across the river, we saw a small stretch of beach all alone with the sun shining upon it. We said some prayers, addressing the spirits and asked the river for safe passage and a fruitful journey. It was very hot and sticky. The river, from this side, seemed much more kind. Just as we were about to launch, we found small eagle feathers, the soft under feathers that this majestic bird may have preened. This was the first eagle feather that we found - an honor and message wrapped in one. Since by tradition the one who finds it is the one that it is meant for, my dear friend embraced it only after explaining to her that it was given to her and was hers to have. Off we went across the river in our inflatable boat. We must have looked reminiscent of a cartoon or an old episode of the Little Rascals! Our combined paddling skills were weak. My friend, at the helm, paddled us in circles. Around and around we went as we crossed the river. Trying to keep a solemn and humble feeling was difficult as we tried not to laugh or make fun of ourselves as we spun towards our destination. Finally we arrived and landed on the beach. The banks on the river didn't look as high from across the way. We needed to find the best route up. Looking around we decided to use an animal path that had been carved out in the thicket by, most likely, a deer. We could not see what was in store for us at the top of the bank and assumed that it was flat and negotiable. Well, as they say, "When one assumes, it makes an ass out of you and me." This place was thick with primitive growth - tall grass, trees large and small, and worst of all, it was covered with briar. "What now," my friend said. We decided to go ahead and follow the deer paths. Not anticipating the terrain, we were wearing only shorts and flip-flop sandals. There was not a clear way ahead and we knew not if we had gotten to the point on the island where the ceremonial ground was. Stopping, we looked back out to from which we came. Behind our point of entry, off in a short distance, lie the Appalachian Trail. Grand, high and beautiful the sun shone brightly upon it. At its highest point, you could see a rock formation, and the colors were different from the surrounding area. A shining copper glow came from the rocks that jutted out past the others, forming a point. 'Wow," my friend exclaimed. "That's Indian Point. We read about it, and not knowing, we parked below it. It has a perfect view of this island." As a matter of fact, if standing there, you could see the island in total including any activity that came up or down the river for miles. There were more reasons than coincidence for why it was this way. The Lenape came from present day Kingston, New York from the North and from Delaware Bay to the South to gather at the sacred island. We knew at this point that we were close to the fields of the encampment and continued to walk through the briars, which had no mercy whatsoever, one or two steps at a time and no more. To our surprise, the island appeared to stop and another river appeared. It was too much to cross, and we were not even sure if this was the end of the island at all. We found an old tree that had turned white and shimmered in the sun and turned towards it. Stopping there, we made our prayers and offerings. Hot and tired, we sat for a bit in silence and made our departure back through the briars, trying to find the right deer path that would return us to the beach. When we found it, we returned to the beach and our inflatable vessel. We rested and didn't speak much. Our legs were torn apart by the briars and bleeding, hundreds of scratches and cuts ran up and down our legs, feet and arms. We went into the river to clean them off. The water felt wonderful, but you could also feel the burn of the injuries reminding you they were there.

We sat on the beach and began to speak. We came to the conclusion that the harsh terrain was there to protect this sacred place. I began to pray silently. I had come here in search of something but not sure what. I prayed for a sign that the ancestors knew my heart, heard my prayers and received my offerings of tobacco and herbs. Earlier, on the way down the bank to the boat, my friend found another small eagle feather. She felt bad that I seemed disappointed in the journey, but in my heart just a little sad. I came with good intentions, compelled if you will. We lied on the bank and enjoyed the solitude for a while. I began speaking again of what I felt in my heart concerning the day. At that point, we decided to leave. While still speaking and getting ready to rise to my feet, something caught my attention in the sand and drew me towards it. I continued to talk and walked in its direction, my friend not knowing what I was doing. Something was buried in the sand looking like a bleached-out bone or a piece of driftwood. It pulled me towards it, almost like a magnet. Still, I was not able to identify what it was. Reaching down, I grabbed its narrow barrel and pulled it up and out of its sandy, shallow grave. "Oh my God," I exclaimed. It was a large eagle feather, a flight feather. I was overwhelmed with emotion. This was the answer and the reward! This was an honor and sacred gift, not only from the bird but from the ancestors. "They heard me, and they acknowledged me." They gave me something that connected me to them, something of their culture that I would recognize as just that. This was a benchmark day!

The thing that made this day even more special and relevant is the fact that this was the feather of a spotted eagle, the eagle that had come to me in days past, the one that would leave an everlasting impression on me - the one that I thought was of only legend and lore. Dots were being connected again. The comfort I felt in my spirit that day will never leave me.

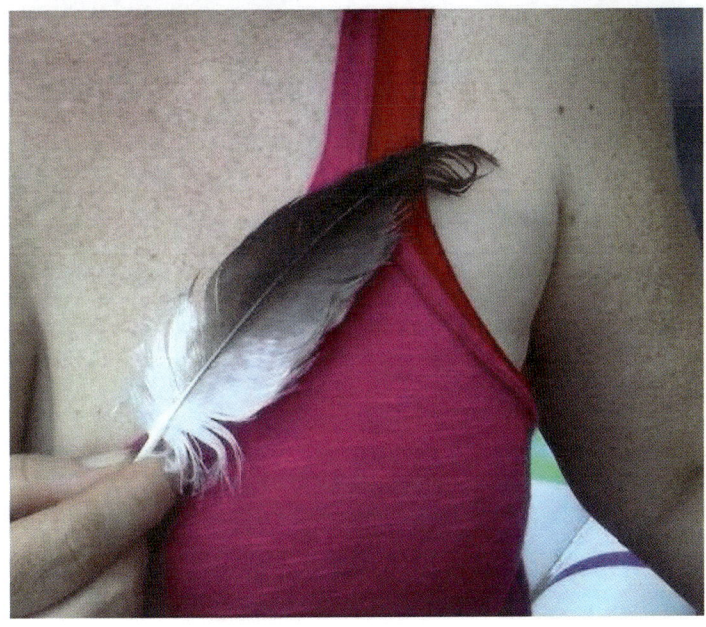

81   THE CROW AND FIRST EAGLE FEATHER

MYSELF AND GIFT OF EAGLE FEATHER

SPOTTED EAGLE OR YOUNG EAGLE

THE ROAD CHANGES

Life along the way took another turn. When I was a younger man of 26, I suffered a back injury that, most likely, had its roots in an earlier incident on a chopper at age 17. By 26, however, I found myself in much pain. This resulted in a trip to the hospital for back surgery. It was my birthday. I stayed in the hospital for ten days. The incurred damage left me out of work for approximately a year and with a partial disability. Prior to, and for the next 24 years, I would make my living trucking.

The damage incurred so long ago led to another series of operations. This time, however, I would have to give up my long time career. The toll taken on me physically was irreversible.
The forecast for the future was one of uncertainty both financially and mentally. No longer would I be out in the mountains bonding with nature. The freedom of spirit that the job on the road held would be gone. The need to find a new way forward was greater than it had been in a very long time.

While recuperating I found ways to keep busy doing small tasks in and out of my home. I began a well regimented diet of healthy foods which resulted in weight loss and positive numbers on blood tests. I continued my daily prayers and looked for the positive in the circumstances I found myself. My closest and dearest friend came to care for me during my infirmary occasionally joined by my spiritual sisters, who also came to check on me and assist in my yard. Those whom I gave to give back. Normally being cast in the role of caretaker, I was not accustomed to having others care for me. In past years there had not been a need for it. This time in my life would be a time of complete change. I welcomed the help concerning my personal needs, and I felt loved and cared for by those whom I surrounded myself with for so long. My dear friend showed me the love and care that I hadn't felt since the time of my childhood and the old Sicilian women. Once again I found myself being cared for by loving and good women. They were strong in heart and spirit, and I trusted them with every fiber of my being. Their willingness to help and their honest concern warmed my heart and touched my spirit.

As I was able to get around a bit more freely, I took advantage of the summer season and sunbathed each day. The warmth of the sun, and the sunlight itself, did wonders for me mentally and physically. Yet there was still a need within me to continue my medicine by helping others, and in turn, helping myself.

My dear friend had a daughter, a beautiful young lady in her teens. I knew her well and loved her, too. She had been in a dream I had years earlier. In that dream, I saw her walking about aimlessly being neither on the ground nor in the sky but somewhere in between. She seemed lost, looking for something or somewhere. Her mom had told me of health issues that she was being treated for. One was a disorder affecting her skin, the other, a type of depression. Much had occurred in her short life on earth but visually seemed well. One treatment she received regarding her skin issue required UV light therapy. It was expensive and short-termed. Her mom requested that I ask her to come and sunbathe with me. The sunlight would help her, and being outside of the confines of her home would as well. We began each day designating a time to be in the sun, regimenting the sunning to resemble a therapy. We spoke and learned about each other. I learned from her young wisdom and she from my life experiences. The time we spent together would evolve into discussing spirituality and the human condition while trying to help her connect the dots in her life. In our conversations, I shared things with her that I had gone through in my youth and how it eventually all ended up making sense in my adulthood. All those experiences helped shape the way that I viewed and reacted to things and how I responded to things in the future. We talked and sunned for a few hours each day. I performed energy medicine and light massage to ease the residual discomfort from her afflictions. Each day we shared a good and healthy meal together, and this brought us closer in our friendship and allowed us to be and speak to each other as two equal beings. Openness and honesty were on the menu.

All was improving with her health and the flare-ups of her condition had diminished. One symptom of her affliction would sometimes leave her feet in a debilitated state making walking difficult. I addressed that issue, as well, to the best of my ability. This was a first for me, but I was willing to give it a go, and she was as well. Many days were spent massaging, soaking, scraping and filing her feet. My heart felt sadness for her. This was just one of the many things she had to deal with during the tender and hard years of her youth.

When all was said and done, my attempts to help her were

successful. Her feet looked and felt great and her skin healthy, but most importantly the state of her being improved. There was still much to work on, but the time we shared was a great step forward. Our friendship continued once summer had past. She continued to grow spiritually and as a woman. In a sense she had become my spiritual goddaughter but will always be my friend. She brought something to me that I needed in my spirit. While I helped her to heal she, in turn, helped me to heal. I am grateful to her mom, my dearest friend, for sharing her family with me and giving me the opportunity to help. I also thank this young woman for helping me and for being part of my life and for her love and for who she is. Our journey together continues, and for now, we will walk together along the way.

Prior to this new way of life the impending circumstances were precursor by other personal sorrow. Two years before ending my career my mother became sick. She faded over the course of time. The zest for life and what seemed to be her will or want to continue made her a mere shadow of her former self. All my life she had been my rock, my conscience and my confidant. She taught me many of values that I hold such as fairness, sticking up for the underdog and being responsible at life and at work. She shared with me an incredible sense of humor and wonderful social skills. She taught me to dance. As I watched her slipping away, her quality of life diminishing, I felt frustration and disappointment. Inside I felt that she had given up, and I reminded her of the lessons of her late husband, my father, that strength and will would carry her forward. Yet she continued to sit each day in a trance-like state staring off into space and ignoring all that was going on around her. The sight of this once strong and vivacious woman slowly fading away was a heartbreaking sight to behold.

While all this was occurring, there were other problems and concerns within my family. The glue that kept us tight weakened, the cloth from which we were made from was tearing apart. I could not imagine how my father would have felt or reacted had he been alive to witness what was happening within his family.
Once a strong, proud and close group, together at each holiday, living in the same neighborhoods and moving to the same areas we were now almost unable to be in each other's company. There were many factors contributing to those feelings and animosities. None were good nor of the values that, to speak for myself only,

were what I remembered being taught. In any case we went forward and did our best to care for our mother, to be close with her, and help her find peace.

The last days of her life were spent not in the home she worked and struggled so hard for but in a rehabilitation facility - at least that is what it was called. By definition, it was a nursing home, a place which she did not ever want to be or visit for that matter. I went to see her when I returned from my work on the road. Some days, she would sit in a common area, other days were spent in bed. Myself and whatever sister was there with me would try to get her to speak, to jar her memory, and keep her alert. Most of the time she was unaware. On the last week of her life, things were a bit different. One day she was completely lucid and aware of whom everybody was, their names, etc. While this was going on we tried to keep her talking and called on the phone those of us who were not in attendance. I tried to get her to speak about circumstances in her home and of her life with my middle sister, suspecting for a long time that something unsavory was unfolding behind the scenes. In the end, my suspicions were proven correct. This was a truly stellar moment of clarity with smiles, laughs, and a final look at my mother that I knew and loved so very much for one last time. Soon after she went back into her almost coma-like state, back to her bed, unresponsive, staring out into space and waiting.

I visited with her just before leaving for a two day road trip. It was bittersweet as I sat beside her bed, holding her hand. I told her it was okay to go and not to worry about her family. If she wanted to stay and fight, that was good, and if not, go and find peace. I told her how much I loved her and how sorry I was for any of my indiscretions that may have caused pain in her life. She held my hand tightly, and though unable to respond, a tear rolled down her cheek. When I told her again how much I loved her, she squeezed my hand more tightly. With a heavy heart I left. Turning towards my sister who was entering the room, I walked by and said, "This is it. I'll never see her again." It dawned on me that she was waiting for something that was inevitably coming and coming soon. She had participated in this so many years ago. Around 2 am the next morning, my cell phone rang while I was asleep in my truck in New England. This was the call I had been waiting for. As I answered, I said, "It's over?" not hello. The reply was "Yes." "I'm coming home." I would remember this day always. It was my birthday.

What would be the next stop along the way, what was to come? Had this journey of purpose peaked? My family, as in the way I knew it to be, would be unrecognizable. The losses of loved ones and the loss of trust, honor and patience and a loss of tolerance, on my part, had taken its toll. I felt lost again but at the same time felt a great deal of pressure released from my spirit.

On the way ahead came a time of renewal. I would, once again, see life through new eyes, separating takers and givers, directing my love and attention to those around me who were there when I needed them, and changing the role I played in my own life as well as the role played in others.

During the summer of recuperation much more became clear. For the first time, I was concerned with my own well-being, future and happiness. Once summer ended and turned into fall, the realities of the road ahead began to consume me. The life I was comfortable in became something of the past. I felt depressed and angry, the anger being fueled by a feeling of uselessness. Concerns about finances, as well as a feeling of disappointment that appeared during the time I required care, also added to my turmoil and simmered away like a slow-cooking stew of emotion. At times it came to boil, and with no one watching the flame, it spilled over and made a mess. Those close to me shared in my frustration and disappointment regarding the lack of care I received. This calloused my heart towards the one who disappointed me. My friend of many years, tried to motivate me to find something to get involved in. She was truly concerned for me and my mental well-being and very aware of the circumstances in which I was living.

In endeavor with a relative was about to come along, something I loved to do and my relative as well. We began to make plans and put them into action. This sparked new life and energy into my spirit. My journey of purpose was to continue. Things were going to happen at the right time. With my financial state depleting, along with my hopes, this would become the way forward. Everything was in place, and we were on our way. I would work again doing something I loved with someone I felt good to be with, a person of whom I held close to my heart and shared blood with. Time was rolling by, and I was growing

anxious and becoming nervous. Nerves gave way to anger, then disillusionment, disappointment, and finally depression. Due to unforeseen circumstances, this project would not come to fruition by no fault of my own or my relations. We were beside ourselves, both feeling the same way. At this time, we needed this to happen- both having the same reasons for needing it only under different circumstances. The day that I called him to tell him I could no longer wait was hard and sad, but I needed to find my way ahead on my own. With pressure on to earn and be purposeful, I began to entertain other avenues. My old friend offered me opportunity in her industry, but at the time, it almost felt like charity, and I declined. I began making calls, going on interviews, etc., not having any good results. My fiftieth birthday was upon me, and the third anniversary of my mother's death.
This date came and went and was spent with all those that I held close to my heart. However, it was not a good day for me though the intentions of those who participated and tried to make it one were honorable.

December came, and still no prospects. I went on an interview but wasn't thrilled with the energy of the place doing the hiring. Being out in search of work was motivating. Three weeks before Christmas, I asked my old friend if there was still an opportunity available at her place of employment. She responded by telling me to speak to her sister, who was the owner of the business, and I did. We talked - her sister knew that I was a friend of the family. Not too long before their mother had passed away. I attended the services for her and found myself alone paying my respects. Unaware of what was going on around me, I said my peace to their mom. When I turned to walk away, to my surprise, everyone was seated. All were watching me. I smiled and said, "Oh, I guess this is going to get started." My old friend glanced up at me from the front row and said, "Since you are up there, you can go ahead and begin. Go ahead - talk." I found myself delivering a eulogy for their mom that I hadn't expected to perform. Being that I knew her and spent time with her in a spiritual way, I was able to do this. Later her sister came up to me and thanked me for such a wonderful speech, saying there wasn't a dry eye. She asked what language I prayed in, and I responded, "Lenape, the grandfather's language."

At the interview I sat speaking to my old friends sister, a woman whose company I had been in before at the home of my friend and also at her wedding. She bestowed an honor upon me when she chose me to walk her down the aisle - the result of a long and emotional journey that I had walked with her, one that started many years before. This was a triumphant day, a day of arrival - a day that new life took root for her and her journey ahead! Our talk was open and honest - she was as professional as she was attractive in her appearance. I smiled a lot and just listened. In conclusion she told me that should would hire me, but at the same time saying "I'm not sure what I'm hiring you for but I feel it inside. There is a reason and purpose for you to be here - you are needed here. I'm just not sure what this is yet, but it will become more apparent as time goes on. I was happy, yet cautious, in my response. "When shall I start?" "When do you want to?" she asked. "What will I do?" "What do you want to do? You will find something here. Just let me think and let me get to know you better as a person. I am aware that you are long-time friends with my sister, and, until recently, didn't know that you were friends with my mother. I love the way that you spoke and presented yourself at my mother's wake. I was truly impressed. Your words and manner had an impact on me that I continue to think of. You'll be fine." I thanked her for her kind words and for the opportunity she was giving me. To do what? I wasn't sure, but grateful in any case. It was just before Christmas, and I smiled and realized that this would be the next stop along the way.

THE ROAD GOES ON

The days at my new career, employed as what I'm not sure of, were going smoothly. I enjoyed the fact that I had someplace to be and something to do with my time. However, there was much internal debate concerning my new place of employment. The working environment was new to me, and some adjustments had to be made regarding my co-workers. Having been a solo act for a very long time, I wasn't used to being surrounded by others - I had been by myself and with those who rode the highways and byways. All I had learned in the past regarding my livelihood would need to be adjusted to a new and different genre, for my journey had taken me to a salon and spa! My co-workers and clientele were, basically, all women. Before accepting this position, I spoke at length with my dear friend and my daughter - in-law and sought their opinions on this new undertaking. I knew both would be honest with me, and their reactions were similar. "You will be in your element. Surrounded by women puts you in your comfort zone....A salon has a social element, and you love to talk, it's perfect!" Perhaps they were right. My partner bad a similar response but many reservations. My partners chosen profession was that of a hair stylist. She had owned a salon in the town that I grew up in. While l was trucking she remained very open to the fact that I had appointments for healing's on the weekends while I was at home - and they were all with women. Some she knew, and those that she didn't she met in advance. Only one issue occurred during this time. The woman that I was going to work on was a hair stylist/salon owner and approximately the same age as my partner. My partner found this unsettling. I worked on her, and after she left, my partner vocalized her feelings. Apparently, she knew more about ladies in that circle than I since she worked in the industry for 31 years.

My new employer continued to guide my way and direct me to the places she felt would suit me. In the beginning, it took time for my co-workers and guests of the salon to warm-up to me. However, the more we spoke, the more they found out about me. They learned of my healing's and beliefs and took interest in them. This allowed them to be more open to my presence at the salon. A few of the girls I knew and had worked on previously. Others attended lectures given by my native friend. Some I was aware of from conversations with my old friend. I continued to search for my purpose in this place. Using the freedom my employer gave me and trusting her feelings and keen sense of people, my role in the salon began to take root. She believed that I would bring good things her way, and I was going to do my best to make that happen.

Finding comfort in my new surroundings was an easy and natural progression; however, in some sense, things in my home became different. I didn't know it, but looking back I now see it was me. I was evolving. This caused changes in my relationship with my partner. I tried to put things into perspective by re- evaluating our time together and approached this in a manner that was not the way of the past. Seventeen years of my life had been devoted to her, and her life had been good, even though she still dealt with issues from her past and current problems. Our needs and likes grew in different directions. My need to grow mentally and spiritually kept me moving forward. Her infirmaries, illnesses and the influence of her siblings kept her stifled. She was trapped between what was and what could be. A few members of her family held harsh feelings towards me. Unfortunately, my partner continued to confide in her family, unable to keep her own counsel. She shared details of our private live - all the negatives, and none of the positives. Her complaints made it appear as though we had a terrible relationship - me the monster, and her the victim. This influenced the opinion of her siblings towards me, and the poison of one would, in time, affect the way the way all thought. This became an unhealthy element in our relationship. Remembering the promise I made to her in the beginning of our time together that I would be the greatest love she knew, I had loved her and cared for her through all her trials and tribulations. After my back surgery, when I needed help with my care, she was not able to assist me. She always had a reason for not helping. This perplexed and disillusioned me. After much soul searching, I came to terms with it. I continued to honor my spiritual contract, but my feelings towards her had changed.

Adding to this time of change was the loss of my beloved pet. She was a beautiful dog, a reminder of my childhood plan. She came into my life while I was still on the road. A waitress that I was friendly with at one of my stops told me about a puppy, four months old, that had been rescued from a shelter by a friend of her daughter. Circumstances changed and the owners of the puppy found themselves unable to keep and care for her. My friend took me to see the dog, and I fell in love with her. My friend brought the pup to work, and on my next trip through the area, I picked her up. From that day forward we became one. I knew that this was meant to be! She spent many years traveling on the road with me. We ate, slept and played together. She was a fixture in my life and in my truck, and also in my neighborhood where she made her own human friends. She was welcomed into their homes where she spent time visiting, playing and eating. I was surprised to learn that this dog was bi-lingual! She understood the language of my spiritual sisters next door. They enjoyed her company and shared with her the cuisine of their culture. She was (and still is) a beautiful spirit. It seemed that my relationship with her needed no words - she could read my thoughts and emotions. With a look, I could read hers as well. She grew sick during the time of change, and this sickness would eventually claim her life. When her time came to go, it was the saddest day of my life. The loss of loved ones, whether family or friends, paled in comparison to the emotional devastation I felt that day. This was the final catalyst to change my life regarding life as I viewed it. Her spirit is with me still and her presence is known on my land and in my home. I planned on having a service for her in my yard, sprinkling her ashes on the spot in the yard where she spent her days watching over her compound. The weather deterred this from happening. Her human friends wanted to attend this ceremony for she had given much joy to them all. I was proud of her in the way the one was proud of their own child. She served a great purpose in my life and in the lives of others, including my partner. I believe she was sent to this place to serve that purpose, not just as a pet, but as a loving, dedicated spirit. In the spring following her passing, I decided to hold a sweat lodge ceremony in her honor. I kept it private with only myself and my dear friend participating. A year prior to this, my dear friend and I had gathered the materials to rebuild the lodge. The old lodge survived through many winters and ceremonies, it's time well-served. As we rebuilt it, we were joined by my spiritual sisters next door, who had also participated in the building of the first lodge. We completed the work, and the following day, it was blessed with a fresh snow. My dear friend and I held the sweat for my pup on the spring equinox - just the two of us. In the past and in the future we would experience much together, in life and in the spiritual world as well. The lodge was extremely hot and soothing. The mood inside was one of reflection, meditation and peace. Growing overwhelmed by the heat and steam and following protocol, we exited the lodge. Lying on the grass, on a sunny yet cool spring morning, we gazed up at the blue sky filled with clouds and tried to catch our breath. I noticed something in the clouds, and I could see it very clearly. My friend, after a moment, turned to me and said, "Do you see it? It1s Tyra! There she is in the clouds." I responded that I saw it but thought, perhaps, that it was just my emotions taking over. There she was, clear as a bell in full detail, right down to her expression.

Another time, while outside speaking with one of my spiritual sisters, she paused in the middle of conversation and looked at the ground behind me. She shook her head, said something in her native language, and walked away. I asked her what was wrong, and she replied, "I just saw Tyra. She was right behind you playing." When I looked down at the ground in the area where my sister spotted her, I noticed one of her old bone toys.

She still comes to me in my dreams.

TYRA

I WILL LOVE AND MISS YOU EVERYDAY OF MY EARTHLY EXISTENCE AND WILL SEE YOU AGAIN WHEN MY TIME COMES TO MAKE MY JOURNEY WEST. WALK IN PEACE...

THE WAY AHEAD

Having been with my employer for some time and even though unclear, my job continued to evolve. My old friend, who was second in command, knew me well, my heart and spirit and all that I represented. Long before I had been there for her. From the time of my own personal and medical issues, she was there for me. Speaking too many in her employ, she diverted some of the tasks she had to deal with in my direction. There was an abundance of personal problems, not so much with the skills and abilities of those employed, but in their personal lives. There were young, aspiring women, seasoned veterans, working moms, and assorted ladies of different ages and issues. The more time spent with them gave me more perspective on how, if I was asked, I could be of assistance to them. Some required help in a spiritual sense, and others needed help achieving their goals in the industry or overcoming issues in their personal lives. My friend informed them about how I her in the past and the strength she drew from our time together. She shared what she experienced and, also, the fact that I worked on her mother as well.

At the same time I was getting to know more about her sister. She was the person I worked for and who gave me what was going to become a wonderful opportunity. We spoke for many hours together, sharing our philosophies, goals and aspirations for the future. I paid close attention to her when she spoke and respected the knowledge she accumulated in business, in her industry, and her ability to read and feel the energy of her employees and guests. She, too, was someone who had a long and hard struggle. However, she stayed with and in the industry that she loved - the beauty business. Though her personal life had many bumps and detours, she stayed true to her calling. The results of her dedication to herself and her convictions had blessed her many times over, not just in a financial sense, but also by how many young women's lives she had touched over time. The ability to see something inside of them, unrecognizable to most, would have her continue to support and nurture them. She did so on a feeling inside and the ability to see past the clouds that surrounded so many of these promising ladies. There were times, though, where she would have to step away, and it would affect her deeply. This to me was inspirational. I recognized these traits as one of a good and kind spirit. She often stated that "in this business you bring peace and happiness to your clients. They come here seeking something, something that makes them feel good about themselves and, in turn, helps them feel good about others and things in their lives." This can apply to any in the personal service industry. These words are wise, true, and speak too many.

We should love what we do with a passion and strive to be the best, not only in a mechanical way, but in the presentation of ourselves, our skills, our understanding, and sheer humanity. "Can you teach an old dog new tricks?" I wondered. Along the way this old dog learned some...

The time spent with my new employer would teach me much and open my horizons. Business is business, but one can still do business with the utmost integrity and passion, not only for the industry in which you thrive but for those to who you lead to their own sense of being and personal success.

As our relationships grew at the salon, more trust and understanding developed between myself and my co-workers. I began to work on them with energy medicine and prayer, making myself available to any and all who needed to speak of things in their lives. I used massage and physical manipulation techniques that I developed prior to the years of my arrival at the salon. The word of the outcome of my spiritual work and energy medicine were reaching to not only my co-workers but to the guests of the salon. They heard positives and began to show interest in my medicine. When I first arrived, due to the fact that I would be in a confined area filled with different types of people and their issues and energy, I found it necessary to do some smudging.

Much had occurred there over the years while it was a functioning and thriving establishment. Many people came and went - employees and guests alike - not all bringing positive energy with them. For myself, my old friend, and a handful of others who had been there for some time, we could feel the weight of that unclean spiritual atmosphere and could see its effects on those who were vulnerable to it. In the years before I came to work there I heard many stories about what had and what was going on. The stories weren't of bad business practices or shabby work; they were of a spiritual matter. Many a clairvoyant, and others with those types of gifts, came in for services. They spoke of heavy energy and of spirits whose energy they felt inside of the building. The moods of the people who worked there reflected the hodge-podge of emotions of those who worked or came there, leaving a stain on the unseen fabric. It is necessary to mention that a place filled with women who still experience their menses also added to the heavy energy. Yes folks, there is a spiritual factor to the menses! It is a personal cleansing ceremony of its own, not only in a physical sense but a spiritual one as well. The energy is heavy and noticeable ,multiple that by a lot, and there you have it! For the benefit of myself and those who worked there and the clientele, the smudging and praying commenced. I performed this quietly and privately twice. After each smudging, I heard comments from the ladies working there - "It seems to be so peaceful here today, very light! Something feels different and very upbeat! Good energy!" Changes in energy and vibration of the salon became noticeable. A greater amount of cohesion in the work force and the way the workers presented themselves to each other and the public were apparent. The departure of those who found pleasure in chaos and drinking from the river of negativity, drama and angst began. They fell from the tree like leaves in the autumn and only allowed the healthy and beautiful colored ones to shine with more vibrancy. The ambiance changed for the good.

I brought a part of the healing ceremonies that I had been doing in my life prior to the salon, minimizing them to fit this genre. There were qualified massage therapists employed here. I began to share with them the things I had done and experienced in my life as a spiritual healer. They were both already proficient in their fields, and what I shared with them served to enhance their skills and abilities. One was of a spiritual nature already. Her own personal story and struggles, however, were keeping her from growing. She had much to offer but first needed to work on herself. The other was quiet and gentle and her energy very comforting. I found them both to be wonderful people, different in their approach and techniques of their chosen profession, but none-the-less capable and talented. The older and edgier I shared my spiritual medicine with, the experiences which brought me to where I was presently. I tried to help her connect the dots in her own life and to try and better understand what and why those things happened in her life. I explained to her how to use them as her personal medicine, and that in the future she would find herself in the service of someone who shared similar experiences with her. She should learn to take the bad that had happened and turn it into a lesson to do good for another. "We're all broken. We are all wounded healers. The pain and the suffering on our journeys serve us in the future. All lessons are sacred, the good, the bad, the ones that make us happy, and the ones that make us cry." How can that be? If you have faith, than you know. All lessons come from the same place. There aren't any coincidences - all things happen for a reason. The difficult part is to self-analyze and discover what those reasons are. "In your case," I told her, "the lessons were to make you more equipped for the circumstances that would arise the more you involve yourself in your calling." The other, more shy, woman, I approached a bit differently. I recognized her presence as being very healing and gentle. She, like all of ns, had issues of her own, yet her energy was caring and motherly. I gave both of them information that would help them going ahead, sharing the healing ceremony that I developed for salon use. I assisted them in using energy medicine not as the way they knew it, but in the way I did. They were both very receptive and eager to continue. I kept my personal spirituality to myself. The way that I proceeded to help another heal was my way and not theirs. They, in time, as I did on my journey, would develop their own methods that they were comfortable with and be most effective at. Going forward, I asked the older one to sit in with me and participate in some of the ceremonies, not all, but ones that would be good examples of spiritual sickness causing physical issues. We worked well together and she was a great asset to the ceremonies and to those who came for help. The quieter one was still a bit unsure of herself in regards to energy medicine. I respected that fact it showed integrity.

One day, while on the floor of the salon, I heard one of the stylists telling a story of what she experienced earlier that morning. This woman was already, in my mind and intentions, someone that could use my skills. I had not approached her to offer my services but my spirit knew it was a matter of time.
Eventually I knew she would come forward, and my opportunity would then be as it was supposed to. Off in the background I stood, listening to her tell her tale. A smile came upon my face as I listened to the details. At a time when the sun had risen, she was out and about walking her dog. It was still hard to see because the sun had not come into full bloom. Her dog began to act strangely, hiding behind her and sniffing the air, pulling her toward the direction of her home. She was unaware of the reasons her pup was so anxious and disturbed. As she stood there, she beard something coming up the street - loud sounds of

of clicking on the pavement. They were moving fast and furious. She did her best to focus her eyes on the area in which the sounds was coming and getting closer. The sun rose a bit more. She glanced down the street, and to her shock and surprise, a very large black bear was running up the middle of the road. The sounds she heard were the sounds of its nails hitting the pavement as it ran. It was coming at her in a rapid pace. Her dog hightailed it, with her in tow, towards home. They reached their door and went inside. She could still see the bear making its way towards her. From the dimensions she gave and her description, it must have been about 500 pounds or more. She watched the bear from inside her home, not being sure of her safety. It reached the corner of her property and stopped. There it sat, looking directly at her. It didn't move nor make a noise, just stared and sniffed the air. At this point, she was completely freaked out and tried to go about her business. Every so often, she looked out the door, and he was still there, staring. Finally, the bear moved on, but not before making a big impression on her and making her quite aware of his presence. This was unusual because it occurred during the time of the year when bears were dormant. Our black bears do not truly hibernate but they are rarely seen until spring. As she ended her story, I walked up to her, smiling. "Do you know why this may have happened? Do you think the bear was trying to tell you something," I asked. She replied, "Not sure, but it scared the crap out of me and was the last thing I expected to happen." I reached for the necklace I was wearing, also known as regalia. It was a large bear claw that I made myself. I said to her, "This is my medicine. I am supposed to work on you now." After a while, when the time was right, I did. Approaching the quieter of the two massage therapists, I asked her to sit in the session with me, thinking it would be a good opportunity for her to observe. She agreed, and the woman being treated agreed as well. Everything seemed to go along. I stayed focused and remained consistent the woman being treated began to move about, displaying discomfort. As the therapy continued, the discomfort grew. I had been using energy medicine on her up to this point, moving down the front of her body, over the chakras. When arriving at the chakra just below the rib cage, she began to vocalize that she was in pain. "I can't breathe, the pain is over␣whelming you have to stop." Staying focused on the task at hand, I continued to work, praying silently the entire time. There was more here than met the eye, a spiritual battle, and I was up to the challenge.

The woman observing sat in silence. Occasionally I would speak to her during the session, explaining how and why I was taking this approach. Finally, the pain and discomfort ceased. I finished up my work, and my client left the room. The massage therapist who sat in with me looked somewhat shaken. "What's wrong," I asked? She replied, "I never experienced something like that before. While you were working on her and she was yelling and moving around, I saw something leave her body. At first I thought it was my imagination, but it wasn't. There was a mist or fog of some sort over her body, lingering in the air, then it was gone." While explaining this to me, she stood next to the door, opening and closing it frantically, trying to create a fan effect to clear the room. "I'm sure whatever that was has gone from here," I said. "That was just way too bizarre for me," she replied. I laughed, "Don't worry - that was just a lot negative energy that consumed her. She will feel better now. She will feel herself again."

Later that day, the woman had an appointment with a client for a haircut and color. She created one of the most beautiful cut and color jobs I had ever seen from her, or from any other, for that matter. This was the work of a true artist, for prior, her work, health, and other things in her life were suffering. She is doing very well now in all aspects of her life. Not all is perfect, but the changes that took place that day made a significant difference. The bear came to visit her again in time, this time as a protector and to remind her to be true to her spirit.

Life at the salon continued to keep me busy - every day an adventure and every day an event! Hundreds of guests patronized it each week. The ladies that I worked with were incredible in their skills and abilities. They were all artists painting their pictures and doing their sculpting on the human canvas. The busier they were the better they performed. For me it was something to behold. I was familiar with this genre, and it never failed to impress me. I witnessed the same type of talent and energy at the salon owned by my partner before we became a couple. Though her business was on a smaller scale compared to the one I would be working at, it was as equally impressive to watch the artistry displayed in her salon. There is a real dedication to the genre by those who make their living at it. As my employer and I discussed with her staff, there is much more brought to the public than just a hairstyle. In my partner's case, career and work ethic kept her vital and her mental health stable. All of the issues that surrounded her life were off the table when it was time to perform at work. No matter the condition of her health, she mustered it up and rarely missed a day.

My own mother was also of this mindset. Outside of giving birth four times, she never missed a day in over 35 years. Two of my sisters also inherited this incredible work ethic. My middle sister, although suffering from advanced Parkinson's disease, would continue to work. When it finally became physically impossible to do so, she worked at part-time at home during the hours her health would permit. During my childhood my friend's moms would be at home and available to serve their needs while mine was at work. On some level, it may have left me flapping in the breeze - no one at home when I returned from school, no cookies and milk served up with a "How was your day son?"

Later in life, I found a great deal of respect for my mom and my sisters and other women that I met along the way who were self-sufficient and able to make their way in life. Their careers and involvement in life outside the home gave them the opportunity to be themselves and to relish the feelings of accomplishment. In away, this kept their spirits free, even when not out and about.

In my case, it served them well and, in turn, served me as well. In my opinion, the responsibilities of being a stay-at-home mom far outweigh the stresses of the working world. It is a job that you rarely get a "day off" from, one that is difficult to take a vacation from and will consume your every thought and every ounce of energy. Again, in my opinion, not worth the pay. A job of that nature cannot be compensated enough, and in many cases, is not acknowledged by those whom you are working for. It is thankless of many levels, and in the end, if the results of all the years of hard work, effort and emotion have not come to be, it can wreak havoc on your spirit. For those moms who endure all there is to endure in their responsibilities in the home and in some cases, the workplace as well, and manage to maintain their health, sanity and ability to smile, my hats off to you!

It was time to revisit the ceremonial ground. Two summers had passed since my last visit, before my change of lifestyle and infirmaries the summer when my dear friend and I received the gifts of eagle feathers from the ancestor spirits. The time to go and pay our respects, to pray for the ancestors, the river, and all who called that place home. We discussed this journey in the spring, and in a way reminiscent of the past, waited for the feeling to come upon us. There is a right time for everything. One beautiful summer morning it came, and off we went. This time the journey did not include an inflatable device. The season bad been a dry one, and we anticipated that the river would be shallow, slow and lazy like hot summer days. We arrived at the same place as the first journey, the original location before the crow called and walked to the river. As we had anticipated, the conditions were perfect, and we decided to walk across. Upon our arrival to the other side, we searched for the entrance to the inner part of the island, the part we weren't able to reach on our last journey, the grounds where once stood the place of encampments, of ceremonies and celebrations. Last time, we made it to the inner river but not the inner island. The water was warm and clear. Again, we found ourselves alone in this beautiful place. We journeyed across the river to the outer bank of the island walking along the edge to the south. As we walked along in the warm and shallow water, we spotted the remnants of animals that had feasted, their prints left in the soft banks and shallows. Piles of fresh water mussels were strewn about. Our relations were eating well. While walking we spoke and reminisced about our last trip here, keeping a close eye on the banks and in the water for signs that would help us find our way. About 1/4 to a half mile down the river, we came upon an inlet. There was a small, sandy beach on all sides, surrounding a deeper pool of water that was clear, yet sandy of the bottom. This would be unnoticeable to those not walking. A small lagoon with the sun beating down on it, the clarity of the water, and the sandy shore was all so very beautiful. We stopped for a moment to enjoy our discovery. At the time we did not realize exactly what we had found - it was the outlet of the river that ran inside of the island. When we moved inland, we recognized it to be. The inner river was a bit deeper and murkier with lots of growth downed trees and limbs blocked the entrance to it. The looks of the terrain surrounding it were similar to the thorny thicket of our last trip. Deciding to go back to the main river, we walked from whence we came. We passed more of the prints and discarded shells. I walked and prayed to the spirits, asking them to show me the entrance to the place I was looking for. I came upon some eagle feathers, maybe three or four smallish ones, and possibly top feathers from the tail or wing. This was the sign I had prayed for - the ancestors' calling card. I picked them up and thanked the ancestors and the spirit of the eagle that had left them there.

Wandering on, passing where we had first crossed, I went ahead of my friend. I noticed a small break in the growth upon the bank another entrance ,again one that had gone unnoticed if not in the water. I climbed up the bank and through the break in the trees. As I looked up, I found myself standing on a wilderness sidewalk of sorts, and open pathway surrounded by growth but clear to walk. Continuing forward - there is was - the inner river! I yelled to my friend, "Come and see. This is incredible, a scene out of a fairy tale." My eyes beheld a shallow river with small pools and sandbars completely covered by a canopy of trees. My friend approached and found this place as enchanting as I did. Together we walked up the bank, just over the crest past the tree line to the inner island. We had arrived! Our feet found themselves on the ceremonial grounds that we had searched for during our first journey. There were acres of open fields lined by trees, almost as a farmers field is lined with a hedge row and field growth thick and tall from ground level up almost six feet. We didn't dare walk into it blindly nor did we have a machete to clear a path. At the edge of a small bill, we made our offerings and said our prayers. Small birds flew about and the sun shone brightly on the field. At the conclusion of our prayers, I asked the ancestors for acknowledgement of our visit with them. No sooner than the words left my mouth, a large burst of wind came over the field and into the trees where we stood. With it came a small swarm of butterflies from out of the field. We took this as our sign and began our departure down the bank of the inner river. Turning to my friend, I said, "I wish they had sent a stronger sign, something that would have told us, without question, that they heard our prayers for them and this place." We stepped back into the water and walked into the middle, looking down at the river bed and continued having conversation. Suddenly, my friend yelled out, "Look - right there, just ahead." I glanced up from the water, and just a few short feet from and a few short feet above us was a golden eagle in flight! Apparently he had been perched there watching us and listening to our prayers. He was large in size and magnificent, the sun reflecting off his golden feathers, illuminating him in his flight. He flew low and straight, not far above the water, and then around a bend. We walked in the water towards where he flew and then he flew across our path and into the ceremonial grounds. This was not a coincidence. The ancestors spoke once again. The eagle was taking our prayers for them to the creator. It was a wonderful and fulfilling day. We would return to this place, once again, that winter, making our journey across in the freezing cold water to pay our respects and offer our prayers.

My life at the salon continues. Every day presents something new to learn. My daily spiritual obligations consist of counseling my coworkers and assisting those that need my help. Energy healing treatments, spiritual cleansing, mind-body-spirit balancing and the sharing of my medicine is something that I practice regularly. I have assisted more than one hundred people with these methods.

My heart and my spirit are full. It is an honor to be able to assist someone in this life with things they find difficult to handle, understand or deal with. Guiding those who are looking to open their hearts, minds and spirits while connecting the dots in their own lives is my journey. Together we set our spirits free, giving us the ability to live in the circumstances that we found ourselves in. Each and every one of us has a story. Each story, though some may be similar, our unique to us like a fingerprint. When we find ourselves wondering why, or maybe a bit misplaced in life but sure that there is as reason we are on this earth, but not able to see clearly what it is, it is time to seek our spirit. This is our own personal journey to discover who we really our and what our meaning and purpose is here on Mother Earth. What is it that we are meant to be, and where do we fit into the web of life?

When we look upon another, we see what our conscious mind allows. We make determinations regarding what this person may stand for or represent, what their social status may be. We make determinations on their appearance and body type. When looking upon a bear, we see a bear. When we look upon an eagle, we see an eagle, a tree a tree, a rock a rock. It is almost as if we were looking at their spirit for what we see is what they are, not much guess work or doubt. Looking at ourselves, we are not what we always appear to be. We sometimes see what we would like to see, but others may not share that same vision. Often we see ourselves in a bad light, obsessed with our body type and visual image. Sometimes we are pleased with what we see, looking with pride and self-admiration. The question is, do we ever look inside to see who our true self is? Do we know and acknowledge our spirit? Can others recognize this in us? Is there a need to take a journey of self-discovery to put all that has happened and all that will into perspective? Will this help me on my way forward to bring out what is inside of me to the surface? These are questions that can only be answered by you. We are physical beings as well as spiritual beings, and life itself is a spiritual journey. "The eyes are the mirrors to the soul," it has been said. Unless you are willing and able to look inside, then you will never know. Life is a circle, and all things in life are a circle as well. From where they start, they will end up again. If the circle you find yourself in spins through generations unchanged and the patterns that have formed upon completion of each circle are the beginning of the next, it may be up to you to make the change. Start a new circle - a circle of growth both mentally and spiritually - a circle filled with love and the sharing of it and care for all things filled with positive attitude and energy. When it comes to completion the next will follow suit. In turn, this will change not only your life but those around you and those yet to come.

Along the way my journey of purpose was unclear at best. The only thing that kept me going was a feeling inside that there was something more that in the future would make sense. As I continue my journey along the way, I looked back not to dwell, but to propel myself forward. What has happened has already happened and now it is done. There is no reason to revisit it. Accepting what was taken from each one of the people who have touched my life, for each of the failures and victories, from all of the smiles and laughter, to all of the tears and heart break has made me what I was meant to be. I will never feel sorry for myself or have any regrets for my life or the course that it has taken. Speaking for myself alone, I believe that this was all predetermined, that my mission and purpose upon this earth was to bring peace to my spirit and to end and not perpetrate the circles that had been started long before my time - the circles that would bring nothing good forward with them. The things I had dreamed of and put into my childhood plan for life have come to be - maybe not in the way I anticipated, but none-the-less. It took thirty two years of life's lessons to pass before the start of my life could begin. It took the next eighteen years to find out and make sense of the first thirty two! This journey has been my own, and I am sure it is not over yet for now, this day, like all in the past, are just another stop along the way.

THANK YOU

FOR TAKING THE TIME TO WALK WITH ME, ALONG THE WAY

WISE WORDS OF TECUMSEH

Live your life that the fear of death can never enter your heart
Trouble no one about his religion
Respect others in their views and demand they respect yours Love your life and perfect your life, beautify all things in your life Seek to make your life long and of service to your people
Prepare a noble death song for the day when you go over the great divide

Always give a word or sign of salute when meeting or passing a friend or even a stranger in a lonely place

Show respect to all people but grovel to none

When you rise in the morning give thanks for the light, for your life, for your strength

Give thanks for your food and for the joy of living

If you see no reason to give thanks, the fault lies within yourself

Touch not the poisonous firewater that makes wise ones turn to fools and robs their spirits of vision

When your time comes to die be not like those whose hearts are filled with fear of death so that when their time comes they weep and pray for a little more time to live their lives over again in a different way

Sing your death song and die like a hero going home

Tecumseh, Shawnee

GOOD BYE

FOR NOW